Holwell Tor quarry and the ruined blacksmith's shop as the artist saw it in 1829. Reproduced from an original print by T. H. Williams by kind permission of the owner, Mr. J. V. Somers Cocks.

DARTMOOR
Then and Now

F. H. (Harry) Starkey

Best wishes

Harry Starkey

First published in 1986
by
F. H. Starkey

ISBN 0 9507240 4 1

By the same author:
Exploring Dartmoor (1980)
Exploring Dartmoor Again (1981)
Dartmoor Crosses & Some Ancient Tracks (1983)
Odds & Ends from Dartmoor (1984)

To the memory of the Dartmoor Giants of the past—Robert Burnard, Sabine Baring-Gould, William Crossing and Richard Hansford Worth, to whom all lovers of the Moor owe so much.

On the publication of this, my fifth book about Dartmoor, as in all the others, I have to acknowledge with grateful thanks the active help, encouragement and companionship of my friends Grace and Les Landon. I must also thank my friend Aileen Carrett who has developed and printed nearly all the photographs used to illustrate this book.

Printed in Great Britain by A. Wheaton & Co. Ltd., Exeter

CONTENTS

FOREWORD

This book contains sixteen chapters, mainly short, about various aspects of Dartmoor which have come to my notice as I have pursued my study of Dartmoor in recent years. My earliest interest in the Moor had its beginnings in the early 1950's and amounted to little more than a fascination with a subject which was then totally unknown to me. Today, looking back over more than thirty years I find that although the years of reading, discussion and active exploration have given me what kind friends describe as an extensive knowledge of the Moor, my real knowledge is miniscule when compared with the many still unanswered questions. It is always so—questions breed knowledge and knowledge breeds yet more questions, and so it will be to the end of time. I hope that the book, and the illustrations, which were mostly taken specially for the purpose, may put a little knowledge in the way of Dartmoor lovers who are in the earlier stages of their exploration of the area. But more than this I hope that it may demonstrate that it is very well worth while to cultivate the "seeing eye". Once the habit of observation is achieved fresh information constantly comes to light, consideration of this brings further knowledge, and so on. Fear not! You will not exhaust the potential and charm of Dartmoor, even though, like some great Dartmoorians of the past, you grow old in the contemplation of its mysteries.

The last comment leads me to consider how our knowledge of Dartmoor has increased in the last century or so. For instance, it is less than 150 years since Samuel Rowe, quoting a friend, conjectured that the lower blowing house on the Yealm was a hermitage containing the remains of a stoup for holy water. It is less than 110 years since that perceptive antiquary, George Wareing Ormerod, stated quite positively that in his opinion Grimspound was a fold for cattle—contradicting Rowe who in 1848 had described the place as an

For references in Paragraph two above to Samuel Rowe, G. W. Ormerod and Col. Ransom Pickard see: *"A Perambulation of the Antient and Royal Forest of Dartmoor"* by Samuel Rowe. 1st Edition 1848. p. 152. *"The Archaeology of Eastern Dartmoor"* by G. W. Ormerod. 1876. p. 16. And: *Transactions of the Devonshire Association, Vol. 79 (1947)* p. 187.

aboriginal village, which is more or less current thought today. And it was as recently as 1947 that Col. Ransom Pickard, writing in the Transactions of the Devonshire Association, repeated his belief that the bank of earth and stones known as the Great Central Trackway was in fact a track dating back to the Bronze Age and perhaps to the Neolithic. Pickard also conjectured that "some of the Devon and Cornish gangs who had worked on Hadrian's Wall may have journeyed this way."

Today we know that the building on the Yealm was a tinners' mill, where tin ore was processed and smelted. We know, or at least accept, that Grimspound was indeed a village, housing people who lived there during the main period of the Bronze Age, say about 1000 BC, more or less. And it is now generally accepted that the Great Central Trackway was not in fact a track at all, but a tribal boundary separating the lands of one prehistoric tribe from another.

But despite the new information gained in recent years there are still great gaps in our knowledge of the background of Man's occupation of Dartmoor. For example, we have no positive information about the dates of origin of the thirteen great stone circles of Dartmoor—the Grey Wethers, the Scorhill Circle and the rest. They are thought to belong to the period when the Beaker Folk used the Moor, say about 2000 BC, but not one of them has been investigated using modern methods—methods which might well produce material that could be subjected to Radio Carbon 14 dating processes. Or to use a different example, there must now be something like eighty buildings or sites which can be identified as having been used for processing tin ore before the end of the 18th century. But not one of these has been scientifically investigated and they become more and more fragmented as year succeeds year and as more and more people clamber about them in search of interesting items such as tinners' moulds, mortar stones and the like. I do not for a moment suggest that it would be desirable or practicable to fence off or prohibit access to these buildings or sites. But I do think that something should be done to extract from a few of them at least such information as they can provide. It is true that scanty records still survive which mention a very few of these places and tell us that they existed as far back as the 16th century. But we know that tinning was taking place on Dartmoor four centuries before that. What is needed is evidence of period and method and this only excavation can provide.

I am aware of and largely agree with modern thought in

archaeology, which is that while everything possible should be done to preserve archaeological remains actual excavation should be kept to a minimum; resort to the spade being reserved for cases where a site is threatened or in other very special circumstances. I believe however that a special case can be made for a limited renewal of active investigation at a few Dartmoor sites. There is a large and ever growing band of enthusiasts who are passionately interested in Dartmoor in all its aspects and particularly in its archaeology. Many of these people have read deeply in the literature of the Moor and have explored its innermost recesses with perceptive eyes and minds. But they are starved of information which can only be provided by scientific investigation. I believe that many of them, perhaps most, would be prepared to subscribe to a fund aimed at providing the means to finance one or two specified projects. These might be, for example, the excavation of one of the so far uninvestigated stone circles, perhaps the one at Hexworthy or that on Bridestowe and Sourton Common. I think too that the excavation of a tinners' mill should come high on the list of priorities. The one at Outcombe, in the Deancombe valley would probably be very rewarding, and so might the lower blowing house on the Walkham river. I am sure that the latter building, despite the several intriguing features which are now visible, still has information of great interest to yield up if properly investigated.

How could such a scheme as I have suggested be brought to fruition? It would of course be expensive, but I am sure that a worthwhile sum could be raised by public subscription. As to organisation; we are at least not short of talented archaeologists, many of whom would welcome such an opportunity. Devon is also fortunate in having within the county several organisations which number among their interests the history and archaeology of Dartmoor. The Devonshire Association, the Devon Archaeological Society, The Dartmoor Preservation Association and the Dartmoor National Park Authority are among them. A consortium formed from the governing bodies of such associations would surely be interested in and capable of staging and managing such a project and bringing it to a successful conclusion. Such an outcome would add greatly to our knowledge of Dartmoor and might produce evidence of national as well as local importance. After all, we do not yet know all there is to know about the stone circles of Bodmin Moor, or Cumbria or Scotland, to name but three areas. Nor have the industrial archaeologists yet been able to tell us all we would like to know about the techniques employed by the ancient metalliferous miners of other areas of Britain. I know, I am sure, there would be difficulties, there always are. But knowledge is priceless and is therefore cheap at any price. Think about it!

LIST OF
ILLUSTRATIONS

Cover illustration Haytor Vale

1

WHICH WAY
DID THE
OLD TRACK GO?

It is well known that for many centuries before the coming of the turnpike roads towards the end of the 18th century, and long before the days of tar-macadam and the metalling of country roads, wayfarers made their way across Dartmoor by a variety of tracks. Many of these old tracks have survived in the shape of our modern roads; others still remain as green tracks across the Moor and some have virtually disappeared, leaving only vague traces to prove their former existence.

Some of the tracks that still remain to us quite clearly date from medieval times or even from the Saxon era. Further back than this I do not think it is possible to go with reasonable certainty. For example, few people today believe in the Great Central Trackway, so beloved of the Victorian antiquaries, who believed it to be prehistoric. Indeed belief in this nebulous route lingered on into the 1940's—see a paper written by Colonel Ransom Pickard, one time President of the Devonshire Association, in the *Transactions of the Devonshire Association, Vol. 79 (1947)*. Pickard, to his own satisfaction at least, traced the Great Central Trackway from Heatree, near Manaton, to the summit of Lower White Tor, overlooking the West Dart about three miles north of Two Bridges. There it ends, and why a track should take a traveller to the summit of a tor in north Dartmoor and there leave him trackless no-one has satisfactorily explained. Certainly there are traces of human activity along the route described by Pickard. To my eye these resemble much more the remains of a flattened wall or reave than a paved causeway, as urged by Pickard.

But today the concensus of opinion seems to be, and I agree with it, that the G.C.T. is really a tribal boundary, laid down to divide the territory of one prehistoric tribe from another. There is a great collection of these reaves on Holne Moor and elsewhere on the Moor and much work has been done on them by archaeologists in recent years. Nor do the Romans seem to have exercised their road building skills upon Dartmoor. Many researchers have sought for Roman roads across the great wilderness but none has been found. It seems certain that the Romans made their way into Cornwall along the northern edge of the Moor and there traces of one of their roads have undoubtedly come to light.

The monastic tracks which connected the ancient monasteries around the Moor have been described by many writers, myself among them, as has the Abbots' Way, alias the Jobbers' Path, and these do not need to feature in the present discussion. But there is one track, clearly very ancient, which continues to puzzle me because of certain contradictory features which exist along its apparent route. I refer to the track which followed, to a large extent, the line of the present B.3212 road from Moretonhampstead to Tavistock. We are told by several knowledgeable writers on the subject that the principal route between Exeter and Tavistock did not pass through Moreton but instead went by way of Chagford. From Chagford the track took a south-westerly route through the lanes, eventually coming out onto the open moor at Tawton Gate, near where Fernworthy Reservoir now lies. Having passed the Heathstone, an ancient bound mark still to be seen, the track continued over Chagford Common and Water Hill, passing behind where the Warren House Inn is today and eventually came out upon the line of the present road just to the east of Stats Bridge, where the Stats Brook passes under the B.3212. This route is borne out by John Donne's map of the County of Devon, first published in 1765, which is still readily available in the County Libraries. It should be made clear here that there also existed a track which passed through Moreton and linked with the one now under consideration, near Stats Bridge. When the turnpikes were constructed the branch from Moreton became the eastern end of the road now designated B.3212 and the Chagford/Stats Bridge section was abandoned.

Continuing from Stats Bridge westward we now have a more or less uncomplicated stretch of road about six miles in length. Here the 18th century turnpike road (and now the B.3212) seem to have followed almost exactly the line of the ancient track. In doing this the track

2

passed the spot where the hamlet of Postbridge now stands and crossed the East Dart river. The road bridge here dates from the days of the first turnpike; not so the magnificent clapper bridge, which the authorities now seem to agree is of medieval date—perhaps 13th century. But I think that there is little doubt that the track antedated the bridge. Have a good look at the river bed in the vicinity of the present road bridge. The site of the original ford and perhaps even some of the original stepping stones can still be seen. It is a strange feature of Donne's map that it does not show the Postbridge clapper or mention any bridge; just a river crossing over an unnamed stream the course of which is not indicated on the map. This despite the fact that the bridge featured on a plan forming part of *Brittania Depicta*, published by Owen in 1720. But map making before the days of the Ordnance Survey was a very imprecise science and many errors and omissions and many anomalies had to be endured by travellers in those days. No doubt they learned by experience.

Having left Postbridge—the hamlet is little more than two centuries old—the old track pursued a moderately uneventful course until it came to a point just beyond Crockern Tor, the seat of the ancient Tinners' Parliament. Here the modern road makes a sharpish turn to the left in order to reduce the steepness of the gradient as the road descends into the valley of the West Dart, which it crosses by means of a modern road bridge. Here too is the Two Bridges Hotel, formerly the Saracen's Head public house, built by Judge Buller in the 18th century. There is no record of an inn here before that. A few yards to the south of the modern bridge the old turnpike bridge still stands, now in the grounds of the hotel. But the presence of these two bridges is not the reason for the name of the place. This is said by the placename pundits to have its origin in the old word *tobrygge*, meaning "at the bridge".

But the track which preceded the turnpike road did not take the route just described. Instead, having passed Crockern Tor, it took a much more direct line down into the valley of the West Dart, which it crossed by means of a ford roughly halfway between the present road bridge and Crockern Farm. Having crossed the river the track mounted the steep incline on the western side, presumably passing to the south of the place where Beardown Farm now stands. Now the traveller was faced with another stream to cross—the Cowsic, and here was one of Dartmoor's most beautiful and picturesque bridges, the Beardown clapper, built to accommodate the wayfarer. This splendid bridge, probably every bit as old as its fellow at Postbridge, has five distinct spans. It is getting on for forty feet long but is only a little over three feet wide. Crossing tells us that the bridge was swept away by a flood in 1873 and badly damaged again in 1890. After the last incident the bridge was rebuilt by the Dartmoor Preservation Association and it is this structure we see today. Beyond the bridge the old track mounted the steep incline and pursued its way westward. But which way did it go? Let us examine the evidence.

Whichever way the track went it had, in the near distance, to negotiate yet another stream, the Blackabrook. The modern road crosses this brook by means of a modern bridge at a point a little over a mile from Two Bridges. One respected and knowledgeable writer, in a recent book, insists that here too the old track crossed the brook. He points to the fact that by doing so the track would be taking the most direct route, which is true. He also points to the presence in the brook, a few yards downstream from the road bridge, of a structure which he identifies as a clapper bridge, wide enough for foot-passengers only. But I wonder?

Examination of this structure reveals that although old it is almost certainly not ancient. I base this theory upon the fact that the

Possible clapper bridge on the Blackabrook, looking upstream.

4

surviving granite imposts which form part of the structure, as well as the great central pier—a natural rock—and other pieces of stonework, all bear the marks of the drill used to split the rock. Other signs of modernity also exist, for example the presence of ironwork in some of the slabs. Note too that the supposed footbridge is only about twelve inches wide—very narrow when the depth and turbulence of the stream are considered. As far as we know, and upon the authority of Richard Hansford Worth, the drill was not used on Dartmoor for splitting granite before about 1803. By that time the turnpike road had come and so presumably had the road bridge and the need for a clapper footbridge, like the days of the pack-horse, had almost passed away. A further point is worth making here. Near the supposed clapper and close to the left bank of the stream will be found a channel which is almost certainly a dry leat. My own belief is that the structure spanning the stream was not a bridge but part of a weir constructed to build up a head of water which flowed down the leat to supply some of the needs of the newly built War Prison. The War Prison at Princetown was commenced in 1806 and completed in 1809. Clearly a supply of water would have been required on site from the beginning of building operations. Equally clearly the several miles of

Possible clapper bridge on the Blackabrook, looking downstream.

5

the Prison Leat as we see it today could not have been completed in the time. But a leat taken off the Blackabrook at the point we have arrived at would probably have supplied many of the immediate needs.

So now we have raised a doubt about the route of the old track. But of course none of the foregoing proves that it did not take what is, admittedly, the most direct line. There is one more important bit of evidence however. This consists of the existence of a two-span clapper bridge which used to span the Blackabrook about three-quarters of a mile to the north of the present road, close to Fice's Well and within the prison enclosures. The spot is approached by a public footpath through the enclosures, so readers can go and have a look for themselves. The bridge in question is at present in a damaged condition, the damage having been inflicted by a flood four or five years ago. The National Park authorities have promised to repair the damage when funds become available. We know that this bridge is ancient and it is mentioned as such in Mrs Bray's *"Borders of the Tamar and Tavy"*, published in 1838. Also we have the old folk-tale of Sir John Fitz and his wife who were pixyled at this spot in 1568 and got themselves out of trouble by drinking the magical water of the nearby spring. For many years past the spring has been known as Fice's Well. It is encased in granite and bears the initials "J. F." and the date 1568. So there must have been an old track crossing the Blackabrook at this spot and if it had not come from the Cowsic clapper and if it was not making for Tavistock, where had it come from and where was it making for?

In considering the puzzle posed above it is essential to remember that the superficial aspect of the countryside around has changed considerably in the last two hundred years or so. Beardown Farm, with its buildings and enclosures did not appear until the late 18th century. The Devonport Leat, which we crossed just to the west of the Beardown clapper, was not engineered until the 1790's and at that time the Tavistock turnpike road had only just appeared and was probably not yet completed. The famous Long Plantation and the prison enclosures on the edge of which it stands were yet to come. Fice's Well was on the open moor and the Blackabrook was a typical moorland stream, its flow still unaffected by its water being taken by the Prison Leat. All these features tend to occlude the view of the terrain and to make extremely difficult the identification of a route which ceased to be used so long ago. Further and finally, it must be remembered that although one wished to travel from A to B it did not

6

always happen that the same route was followed throughout on every occasion. Dartmoor streams are notoriously quick to rise after rain and in such a case it must frequently have happened that whereas it was possible, even easy, to cross a stream at a given point at 2 pm, the same stream was impassable at the same spot at 4 pm. If this happened the experienced traveller would probably anticipate the situation and veer off his course so as to bring him to a crossing place further upstream. Or, if he arrived at his intended crossing place too late to cross there he would turn upstream to find the next place where he could cross. This is instanced by the famous case of the inhabitants of Pizwell and Babney who in 1260 petitioned the Bishop to be allowed to go to Widecombe church instead of their own parish church at Lydford; because, they said, Lydford Church was eight miles further from their homes than was Widecombe, in fair weather; if the weather was foul the difference was fifteen miles. Which has to mean that if the streams were in spate they could not use the most direct route but had to travel further upstream before they could cross.

So which way did the old track go? I think the answer lies in the final argument above. I think that people used the most convenient route which took them most quickly and comfortably to their destination. So in fine weather they went by the route finally adopted by the turnpike builders and crossed the Blackabrook by ford or stepping stones or clapper bridge, if there was one. But if the weather was bad and the streams in spate they used a different route which took them upstream to the clapper bridge near Fice's Well.

Whichever means he took to cross the Blackabrook the traveller would eventually have to face the Walkham, a much wider river. In the ordinary way he would cross at a ford near where Merivale Bridge now is, or perhaps a little further downstream near Longash Farm. But if this was impossible I have no doubt that there was a crossing place north of Merivale. Using this and adjusting his course accordingly the traveller would eventually rejoin the main track somewhere on Whitchurch Down and complete his journey to Tavistock along the track with which the one from Exeter had now merged. This track, or one arm of it anyway, coming from the vicinity of Buckfast, has for two centuries at least been known as the Abbots' Way and before that as the Jobbers' Path or the Jobbers' Cawse.

2

EPHRAIM'S PINCH

A critic reviewing one of my books described me as "an author who delights in the moorland curiosities". In view of the scanty nature of the review and the context in which the comment was made I think this was intended as an accusation of trivialness. But whether this is so or not I am happy to plead guilty to the charge. Curiosities interest most people and their study can lead to discoveries of much greater importance. It should be remembered too that curiosities can include people, and that nature provides nothing more curious than Man. My mother used to say, "There's nowt so queer as folk."

The Dartmoor scene has thrown up many interesting characters— and continues to do so—and one of the most outstandingly interesting of these was Jonas Coaker, the "Dartmoor Poet". I described this worthy at some length in my *"Odds & Ends from Dartmoor"* and included some of his verses. This being so I will here only remind the reader that Coaker was born of Dartmoor working-class stock in 1801 and died in 1890. He lived all his life upon the Moor and in his time filled many roles—farm worker, wall builder, inn-keeper, rate collector and poet. I recently came into possession of one of Coaker's poems previously unknown to me, and this is reproduced below.

This poem is itself a curiosity in that it provides a very different version of a well known Dartmoor folk-story. Oddly too, the story was clearly the origin of a very strange Dartmoor place name.

Ephraim's Pinch is the name given to the steep little hill half a mile west of Grendon Cottage on the road from Widecombe to Postbridge. It has even found its way onto the modern $2\frac{1}{2}$ inch Ordnance Survey map of Dartmoor. According to Sabine Baring-Gould the name was already on the map in 1809 when the first O.S. map of the district was published. In his *"Dartmoor Idylls"*, published in 1896, Baring-Gould tells the story of Ephraim Weekes, a young farm worker at Runnage, a very ancient moorland farm near Postbridge. Ephraim fell in love with his master's daughter and she with him. But father disapproved and applied delaying tactics. After some years however he agreed that the couple might marry provided that Ephraim could carry a sack of rye from Runnage to the mill at Widecombe, there have the rye ground into flour and return with the flour to Runnage.

I don't know how much Ephraim's sack weighed, but in my day a sack of oats weighed 168 lbs, a sack of wheat 224 and a sack of rye 252 lbs. However, spurred on by love Ephraim accepted this formidable challenge and set out for Widecombe with his sack of rye. He reached the mill, the rye was ground into flour and the return journey began. All went well until he reached the foot of the hill previously described and here he "felt the pinch" and fell on his knees. However, he recovered sufficiently to finish his journey to Runnage, but here, the farmer still refusing to honour his bargain, Ephraim gave up the ghost and died on the spot—of a broken heart, or of exhaustion—who knows?

Coaker's verses tell a very different story. According to this a somewhat similar challenge was issued, but it arose from a boasting session among the young bloods of Widecombe, meeting on the village green one day; one could hedge better, another could plough straighter and so on. Ephraim boasted of the great weights he could carry and was challenged to carry a sack of corn from the village to Postbridge and accepted the bet. According to Coaker the distance is "a good five mile, if a single inch". This is just about right, as the crow flies. But Ephraim was no crow and the nearest practicable route would have covered a distance of about 6 miles. Again all went well until the steepest part of the rise was reached and here the pinch became too much for Ephraim. He flung down his sack upon the road and that was that.

I have the highest possible opinion of Sabine Baring-Gould as a story-teller, but I much prefer Jonas Coaker's version of this old story; it has a ring of truth about it. I very well remember, as a lad working on farms in Lincolnshire, the boasting that used to go on in the stables and the pub. I remember one young fellow, in the pride of his manhood, betting ten shillings that he would carry a quarter of a ton of wheat (two and a half sacks, lashed together) a quarter of a mile. And he did it—albeit on level ground. But Baring-Gould's folklore, like his archaeological reconstructions, is very suspect. He had too much of the romantic in him to be reliable.

Jonas Coaker's cottage as it was in 1892.

Jonas Coaker's cottage at old Ringhill, as it is today.

10

The illustration that accompanies this chapter is reproduced from one used to illustrate an item which appeared in the *English Illustrated Magazine* in March, 1892. The item was entitled *"Amongst the Western Song-men"* and the author was the Rev. Sabine Baring-Gould. The artist is unknown, at least to me, though what appears to be his monogram is seen in the picture, bottom left-hand corner. Baring-Gould was a man of many interests, one of these was Dartmoor, especially its archaeological features and its folklore. He was also passionately interested in old country songs, which he pursued wherever they could be found. He was responsible for rescuing many of these old songs from oblivion by tracking down old people who could sing them. He then reduced the words and music to writing, in may cases the first time this had ever been done. Several of the songs appear in Baring-Gould's *"Songs of the West"*. This was first published in 1889 and is still highly thought of and sought after today.

We visited Ringhill Farm at Postbridge where Jonas Coaker died in 1890, not long ago. We found to our great pleasure that Jonas's cottage is still standing, if in a changed and dilapidated form. The present occupant of Ringhill very kindly allowed us to visit and inspect the old building which lies some distance behind, that is to the west, of the present farmhouse. The cottage has been altered by taking down the front wall, widening the gable-end and then re-building the front wall minus its windows. The chimney stack has disappeared and the interior of the house has been gutted, including the fireplace, though it is possible to see where the latter was. The cottage seems to have been used as a byre or stable. When these alterations were carried out is unknown but it was interesting to find that another building now stands at right-angles to and to the right of the old cottage as seen in the picture. This building is only one storey high, but the three distinctive windows, from the first floor of the old cottage, with their chevron shaped granite drip-mouldings, have been installed in the later building.

EPHRAIME PINCH

Did ee ever yer tell of Ephraime Pinch,
Way up nigh Grendon Cot
There's a clump of virs, and a gate hanged up
By which you may know the spot.

Its a good mile an half, from Runnage Bridge
Ess more'n that I should say
And a monshus place fer rabbits, you'l vind
If ever you pass that way.
Tis close home by Soussons Warren you know,
And that be the cause of they.
Ned Coaker to Hex'ry, he was the fust
That tell'ed the tale to me. And
If twas nort but a passel of crams
You really must'n blame me;
But, I zim it be true, ver in Widdecombe Town
I've eeard the story too.
There's some there, that tell ov the strong man eet,
And the job he tried to do.
And they say if it had n'a bin fer the Pinch
He surely wid a pulled dru.
Nigh Widdecombe Ephraime lived they tell
And all was proud of he,
For the loads he'd pull and carry with ease
Twould frighten ee most to see.
And under such loads he'd never give way
For he was as firm as a poss,
A yaffle of turve he could fling pon the vire
Volks said he was strong as a hoss.
Tis said dree, or vour, a min meet pon the green
And pitched to tell one day what each could do
And from what was said, there was none could work like they
One could datch, and tother could hedge
Wi any man they meet,
Another could plough, like nobody else,
He's furrows was so straight.
Upon their showing; they all had sense, and
Was mortal hard to bait.
It zims that Ephraime was there too and
Said it true might be,
But well he knawed there wad'n one
Could carry a weight like he.
Then up spake one, and said he'd bet, he
Could'nt carry a sack of corn, from
Widdecombe Town to Post Bridge pon his back

A good five mile, if a single inch
And none too smooth a track.
Well Ephraime, he took it up at once,
And they fixed upon the bet
Thin every man went vore to the barn
The sack of corn to get.
Some would have made a bit of a stoor
To rise'n, bless yer heart, but
Twas nort to he, so pon his back
He fling'n purty smart.
So off they go, twould have done ee good
To see min at the start,
He said he feeled as fresh as a lark
I dare say that was true.
But he wad'n so fresh, before he was dru
He'd a toughest job, on setting out, on
His long and toilsome tridge,
The hill was stickle, like the roof of a house
But, he climbs up over the ridge
Then down gore hill, he went like a flash
Till he come to Blackadon Bridge.
Twas slowish work to reach hill head
Then down the steep he passed
Some thought he'd win, but others said they
Didn't think twould last.
He crossed the stream at Grendon Cot or,
Where the Cot now be,
But as he moved vore to the steepest pinch
Twas plain enough to see
The long dree mile that he'd a done
Was quite enough for he.
Ess the pinch was too much for Ephraime,
Wi such a heavy load,
He could'n carry any further, so
He flung'n pon the road.
He carried as long as possible, for
He wad'n a man to flinch
So from that the place have long been known
By the name of Ephraime's "Pinch".

3

CHARCOAL
FROM PEAT

In some parts of Dartmoor many square miles of the moor are covered
with peat which in places is between six and twelve feet in depth. In
some smaller areas the peat may be found to be as much as 20 feet in
depth. This peat, the partially decayed vegetation of the moor, has
been forming since prehistoric times and for centuries was the staple
domestic fuel of the neighbourhood; of this more later.

However, upon the high plateaux of northern Dartmoor, especially
in the vicinity of Hangingstone Hill and Watern Tor and Wild Tor and
above the valley of the East Dart, will be found large areas of land,
many of them several acres in extent, where the peat has been entirely
stripped from the surface. Here the granite boulders show through like
the whited bones of a defeated army upon its abandoned battlefield.
Here practically nothing grows, for man, aided and followed by
natural erosion, has left no soil to give any plant sustenance. In the
vicinity of many such areas the Dartmoor explorer who seeks may
come across the scanty ruins of a few small buildings, clearly of very
primitive construction. These are almost certainly the shelters of the
peat cutters of long ago. He may also find great heaps of peat, many
feet high and wide, which have at some time in the long distant past
been piled up to dry and await processing which never happened. Here
and there too there exist assemblages of granite blocks and boulders of
considerable size which have clearly been arranged for some purpose
other than as buildings. These are thought to be the sites of the
primitive kilns where charcoal was produced from peat by a process of
controlled combustion.

The objects and indications described above are part of a little
known aspect of the tin-mining industry of Devon and Cornwall. One

Supposed site of kiln for making peat charcoal—near Wild Tor.

Ruins of peatcutters' shelter, below Hangingstone Hill.

of the great difficulties experienced by West Country tinners was the absence of suitable fuel with which to smelt their ore. In those far off days—we are talking of the 13th century, perhaps even earlier—coal was not to be had in the South West peninsula. In the absence of coal (or the coke made from it) the next best medium was charcoal made from timber, since timber *per se* could not produce a hot enough fire for smelting purposes. But timber was always in short supply in the tin-mining areas of Devon and Cornwall and with the advent of the tin-mining boom of the 14th century supplies of timber were obviously very strained, even to the point of endangering the very existence of the industry. Who it was that first discovered that charcoal could be made from peat is not known, but it has been suggested that the practice originated on the Continent. Perhaps the discovery was made by accident, or perhaps by experiment born of desperation. What we do know is that as early as 1219 the King, Henry III, issued instructions that the tinners of Devon were to be allowed to take "coals" from Dartmoor for the Royal Stannaries, "as they were accustomed to do", implying that this was a practice of long standing even then. For the next two centuries or more there are further references to this practice and in 1456 Edward IV granted the tinners of Cornwall permission to enter at will the Forest of Dartmoor and there dig and prepare turves for coals and take them away to the King's Stannaries in Cornwall. The document giving this permission recites that supplies of fuel in Cornwall were now so sparse that it could not be obtained in sufficient quantities or at reasonable prices and that the coinage of tin in the county had fallen drastically in consequence.

15

At this point it perhaps ought to be said that peat charcoal is described as being a hard, clean, blue-grey charcoal, resembling ordinary charcoal but considerably lighter in weight. It is said to have a high calorific value, i.e. it gives off a good heat. One hundred pounds weight of air-dried peat is required to produce 36 lbs of charcoal. It is also said that specimens of this charcoal can easily be found on the Moor in the vicinity of the operations described. I have to confess however that I have not so far found anything that I could positively identify as peat charcoal; I shall keep trying.

How long the use of peat charcoal in the tin-mining industry of Dartmoor went on seems not to be known. By the late 18th century the number of smelting houses on Dartmoor had been greatly reduced and it seems likely that the use of coke from sea-borne coal supplanted charcoal about the turn of the 18th/19th centuries. But we know, because contemporary records exist, that peat charcoal lingered on in the countryside around the Moor until well into the 19th century. It is said that local blacksmiths preferred it because, lacking sulphur in its make up, it was better for manufacturing iron and tempering edge tools. Conversely, it is fairly certain that coke was used at the last tin-smelting house to operate on Dartmoor. This was at Eylesbarrow, between Princetown and Sheepstor, and the ruins of the house can still be seen. This smelting house had two furnaces. One of these was a typical Dartmoor "blowing" furnace, in which the fire was urged by bellows, of the kind used in Dartmoor smelting houses for centuries. The other was a reverbatory furnace of much more modern type. The Eylesbarrow smelting house seems not to have operated as such after the early 1830's; the mine itself closed down in 1852 when all the plant was sold by auction. I was present some years ago when a quantity of coke was found beneath the ruined masonry of the Eylesbarrow smelting house.

Of course, peat cutting for domestic and industrial purposes went on for many years after peat charcoal left the Dartmoor scene. In fact industries were founded upon it, for example the extraction of naphtha for lighting and similar purposes, and the manufacture of gas to light the prison at Princetown. But all these and others failed in due course, leaving only the use of peat as domestic fuel to remind us of its long history. Now this too has almost disappeared; just here and there one finds upon the Moor a peat-tie still in use, with a rough track leading away from it which if followed brings one to a moorland residence with a wisp of blue smoke issuing from its chimney and a tang of

16

Cutting peat for domestic fuel—Dartmoor 1985.

burning peat upon the air. The disused peat-ties also of course remain, hundreds, perhaps thousands of acres of shallow rectangular depressions in almost any part of the unenclosed moorland. Half full of water and beset with tangled heather and bilberry, they remind the walker that on Dartmoor a track, even an indirect one, is worth its weight in gold.

FURTHER READING FOR THIS CHAPTER.

For much valuable information about the formation of peat and its use for making charcoal see *"Dartmoor"* by Richard Hansford Worth, privately published in 1953 and now again in print by David & Charles, Newton Abbot.

See also *Devon & Cornwall Notes & Queries, Vol. XXX, Pts. IV & IX (1965 & 1967)*. Notes by Diana Woolner and John Roberts.

In *Transactions of the Devonshire Association, Vol. 106 (1974)*, pages 289–328, is a most interesting and valuable paper by R. M. L. Cook, T. A. P. Greeves and C. C. Kilvington. Entitled *"Eylesbarrow (1814–1852)"* this contains a mass of fascinating information about the Eylesbarrow mine, including a description of the furnaces in the smelting house.

4

PRINCETOWN

It has become a habit, indeed almost a custom, among Dartmoor lovers to speak and think of Princetown in terms of denigration. It is that bleak ugly place, neither town nor village, through which one has to go to reach more interesting places to the north or south. It is a place where one can procure petrol; where there are public toilets and public houses and the odd shop or two where useful items can be bought in an emergency. It is full of trippers who have come to gawp at the prisoners, the prison officers and the prison itself, and who flock into the gift shops and eat ice-cream until it is time for their coaches to take them away again. The place has a wretched climate, with an average annual rainfall of around 80 inches, and when it isn't raining the area is frequently enveloped in dense mist. All these assertions, and more, are true, and the fact that many modern small houses, once occupied by prison staff now stand empty for months on end is a fair indication that Princetown is far from popular as a residential area. All in all it is an extraordinary place whose presence in the centre of a National Park can only be described as anomalous. But there is more to Princetown than appears on the surface, as we shall see.

For example, its history. In a county like Devon, the history of whose towns and villages frequently goes back a thousand years or more, Princetown is almost a newcomer. When Sir Thomas Tyrwhitt arrived on the Dartmoor scene in the 1780's there was nothing on the site of Princetown at all, as far as we know; except perhaps the ancient clapper bridge over the Blackabrook, at the Ockery, just north of the village. That bridge is still there, a splendid and picturesque specimen of its kind which carried the track which is now the B.3212 road from its junction with the Exeter/Tavistock track at Two Bridges to give access to the villages around Walkhampton and on towards Plymouth. We do not know the age of these old bridges but the oldest clappers may be of 13th or 14th century vintage.

Ockery clapper bridge, Princetown.

So Sir Thomas adventured into the wilderness of Dartmoor. He built himself a mansion which he called Tor Royal—it still stands on the outskirts of Princetown. And he enclosed thousands of acres of open moorland with the intention of farming the land. Sir Thomas and many others like him believed that by hard work and intelligent husbandry even Dartmoor soil could be made to bear lucrative crops and they spent vast fortunes in an attempt to prove it. We now know that they were wrong and that the proper use for Dartmoor land is to graze cattle and sheep; but we have to admire their courage and persistence in the face of repeated failure. It was the activities of men like Sir Thomas which were responsible for the existence of the miles of stone walls which border the roads in the vicinity of Princetown.

One of the things that Sir Thomas did in his attempt to put Dartmoor on the map was to persuade the Government, through his friend the Prince Regent, to build a prison large enough to house thousands of French prisoners of war who were at that time incarcerated in hulks moored off Plymouth in conditions of the utmost squalor. The Prince Regent—he later became King George IV—was of course also the Prince of Wales and Duke of Cornwall. In his latter role the Prince was Lord of Dartmoor and owned the whole of the ancient Forest of Dartmoor. The site chosen for the War Prison, which later became known as Prince's Town, occupied a position right on the SW edge of the Forest and consequently the Prince became the landlord of the War Department who leased the land from him as Duke of Cornwall. This is still the legal position today and if the prison is ever closed, as has been suggested from time to time, the site will revert to the Duchy. Work began on the new prison in 1806 and by the spring of 1809 the building was far enough advanced for the first batch of prisoners—2500 of them—to come up from Plymouth, having marched across the Moor. A similar number followed in June and by the time the war ended with the defeat of Napoleon no less than 9000 prisoners, French and a smaller number of Americans, mostly sailors, were incarcerated at Princetown. The war ended in 1815 and the last of the prisoners left the following year. After this the prison stood empty for a while and then, for a short time it was occupied by a commercial undertaking involved in processing peat cut from the Moor. Eventually, in 1850, the old War Prison became Dartmoor Convict Prison and here, for over a hundred years many of the most desperate criminals in the country were kept under lock and key.

The category of prisoners detained at Princetown has changed in recent years but I very well remember, as late as the 1950's, the familiar sight of a mounted prison warder armed with a carbine, keeping guard over a gang of convicts working in the prison fields.

During the currency of the War Prison Princetown burgeoned. Houses were built and shops and public houses were opened to serve the large population of soldiers, who acted as guards, and civil servants attached to the establishment. A market was opened in the prison itself and country people from places as far afield as Tavistock and Holne flocked in to sell their produce to those prisoners who had cash to buy it. Then the war ended and the prisoners went home and of course the village went into a decline—a community cannot make a living by taking in each others' washing. In an attempt to stem this decline Sir Thomas Tyrwhitt and other influential local people obtained an Act of Parliament authorising the construction of a railway connecting Princetown with Crabtree, just outside Plymouth. The Act is dated 1819; it was followed by two others and eventually the construction began and was completed as far as Princetown in 1827. From its inception until 1889 traffic on this line was drawn by horses; it was a goods line only, the commodities carried being quarried stone, lime, timber, fuel and so on. The track was relaid and in 1889 the line went over to steam; passengers as well as goods were carried. But the line never prospered and eventually, in 1956, it closed down. Soon all the tracks were taken up and many of the bridges demolished. Today only the bed of the railway remains. This can be followed, from just outside Princetown, for several miles across the Moor, past deserted granite quarries and skirting King Tor, Swell Tor and Ingra Tor, with marvellous views of some of South Dartmoor's most splendid scenery.

Today Princetown is as you see it, but beneath the surface there is more than you would think. Most people content themselves with a visit to one or two gift shops and perhaps a stroll up the main street as far as the prison entrance. Here stands the massive portico, constructed from monolithic blocks of granite. Over the arch is an inscription in Latin—"Parcere Subjectis"—"Pity the Vanquished", a relic of the days of the War Prison. To understand how much that pity was needed read, for example, Eden Phillpotts' *"The American Prisoner"*, one of his best novels and written at a time when old people could still remember what their parents had told them of the early days of Princetown.

On the opposite side of the road from the prison stands Princetown Parish Church. A large granite building in the Perpendicular style, architect unknown, it was built in the days of the War Prison by

Princetown church.

Memorial cross, Princetown churchyard.

21

prison labour. The French prisoners were largely responsible for the masonry and the Americans made and installed much of the woodwork. Its building provides a dramatic episode in *"The American Prisoner"*, already mentioned. Dedicated to St. Michael, the church is a somewhat plain building. One puzzling feature is that the internal masonry consists largely of limestone. This cannot have come from Dartmoor and it must therefore have been brought to Princetown by rail, long after the prisoners of war had left. When the church was built it was intended as a Chapel of Ease for the benefit of the residents of Princetown because their parish church at Lydford was so far away, nearly nine miles as the crow flies, much further by the nearest practicable route. But later in the 19th century a new ecclesiastical parish of Princetown was created and the church then obtained its present status. As a matter of interest the Civil Parish of Lydford, with Lydford Parish Council as the lowest tier of local government, still covers the whole of the ancient parish and is in consequence the largest of its kind in England. In the church is a mural monument to the memory of Sir Thomas Tyrwhitt, the founder of Princetown.

There are several items of interest in the churchyard, among them a plaque to the memory of "Three Gallant Soldiers" of the 7th Royal Fusiliers. The soldiers, a corporal and two privates, perished in the snow in February, 1853, near Soldiers' Pond, on the common just outside Princetown while returning to their place of duty at the convict prison, before the days of civilian prison staff. Also in the churchyard, to the north of and a few yards from the tower, is a tall and massive granite cross. This must be at least 12 feet tall and is of somewhat formal appearance. It bears no inscription at all but at first glance one might take it for a War Memorial, or something similar. Enquiries however brought to light an interesting story. It appears that from the earliest days of the convict prison, convicts who died in prison were buried in unmarked graves within the prison walls. But in 1912 that rather inhuman policy was changed and from then onward those prison inmates who were so unfortunate as to die during the term of their sentence were buried in the churchyard and this practice is still continued today. The graves of these men are marked by short granite posts, each engraved with the initials of the deceased and the date of his death. These can be seen on the north side of the churchyard, in four serried rows beneath the trees. In 1912 the cross referred to earlier was made by prison labour and erected where we

Convicts' graves, Princetown churchyard.

see it now, in memory of the prisoners who lie in unmarked graves. The sentiment behind this gesture is surely one of which all must approve; at first glance the absence of any inscription on the cross may strike one as unusual, but perhaps in view of the history of the thing matters are best as they are?

As the visitor leaves the churchyard by the main gate he will probably turn right along the street. If he does this he will find, on the opposite side of the road, a little way along, a row or terrace of small houses, about a dozen or so, called Hessary Terrace, each with its own small front garden. Stop and look carefully at these houses; they are striking in the perfection of their proportions and the simplicity of their design. To add to their pleasant appearance is the fact that each cottage retains its original cast-iron railings, though how these escaped the melting pot during the last war nobody knows. These cottages appear to date from the early years of the present century and are among the most pleasant sights to be seen in Princetown today. But there are many other interesting and fascinating items to be found in Princetown by the discerning visitor. I hope their pursuit and identification gives you as much pleasure as it still does to me.

5

HOLWELL TOR QUARRY SHELTER

Among the most fascinating industrial remains to be found on Dartmoor are the sites of several disused granite quarries. Those in the vicinity of Haytor and at Foggin Tor, Swell Tor and King Tor, all near Merivale, are particularly interesting, extensive and easy of access.

All the quarries mentioned above have been extensively written up by Dartmoor authors (see the notes at the end of the chapter) and it is therefore unnecessary to say very much about their general history. Suffice it to say that the demand for high class building material which gave birth to these quarries stemmed from the industrial revolution and the consequent rebuilding of the towns and cities of England and the expansion of trade that went with it. Dates are a bit uncertain but it seems that the earliest of these quarries was not opened much before the turn of the 18th/19th centuries. The Haytor quarries, it is said, have not operated as a going concern since the 1880's, although a block of granite for the County War Memorial was removed in the 1920's. Granite quarrying lingers on to this day at Merivale, though on a very reduced scale. Foggin Tor, Swell Tor and King Tor quarries had all closed down by the late 1920's.

However, this chapter is supposed to be about the Holwell Tor quarry, which is part of the Haytor complex. Haytor is almost certainly the best known of the Dartmoor quarries and has many interesting features to offer. Among these is the well known granite tramway, whose tramlines are made from lengths of worked granite and along which the quarried stone was conveyed the seven miles to the head of the Stover Canal at Teigngrace. There are besides, the sites of two "villages", which provided accommodation for the quarrymen and their families; five quarry sites, large and small, and a number of ruined buildings connected with the industry. Among the latter are two of particular interest at the Holwell Tor quarry. The first of these will be found on the left of the tramway as one approaches the quarry from the east. It is very ruinous, only the two end walls and part of the rear wall having survived. At the back of the building, but inside, is a heap of masonry rubble which is clearly the remains of the chimney stack which must have fallen many years ago. I first noticed this building about 30 years ago and on making enquiries of local people was told that it was thought to have been a public house which existed for the benefit of the quarrymen who were apparently notoriously thirsty people. Some years later, about 1978 in fact, further information came to light which seems to positively identify this building as something other than a pub. This information came in the shape of an old print, dated 1829, a copy of which forms the frontispiece of this book. The print shows a building, clearly the one now under discussion, tucked into the hillside and overshadowed by the quarry-face of Holwell Tor quarry. Leaning against the front wall of the building the artist has depicted an object which is obviously a large pair of blacksmith's bellows. The leanto roof of the building is thatched and the chimney stack, now collapsed, is also shown. The building as the artist saw it was plainly not a pub and the presence of the bellows outside led me to think that it was much more likely to have been a blacksmith's shop. So we went and had another look, and sure enough, by moving one or two pieces of the fallen chimney we were able to discern, beneath the rubble, the flat raised platform of the blacksmith's hearth. Further investigation revealed the fact that there had been two hearths, side by side and that each hearth had been served by a separate bellows; the round ducts through which the air was forced into the furnace are still there to be seen today. But please be content to just look, these old buildings are very fragile and will not stand pulling about.

The second interesting building at Holwell Tor is the quarrymen's shelter. This little building is in quite good condition and stands on a tiny plateau below and to the north of the tramway and quarries. The hut stands about 6ft. high and is roughly circular in shape and about ten feet in diameter. It is of massive granite construction and although the roof appears to be covered in rubble, giving it a beehive-like appearance, this is deceptive because the rubble has in fact been piled

Holwell Tor quarry shelter.

upon a flat roof constructed from a number of great granite imposts. There is no doubt in my mind that this hut was built to serve as a refuge for the quarrymen when blasting was taking place at the quarry nearby. A close examination of the quarry-face will reveal the deep grooves in the rock into which the explosive was packed. In those days the explosive would almost certainly have been "black powder", a coarse form of gunpowder.

The quarry shelter just described is a well known feature to many local people, but it seems to escape the notice of many visitors, perhaps because it is sited below the level of the tramway. Indeed a number of well known Dartmoor writers seem to have missed it altogether—at least they do not mention it. To make sure you find it follow the granite tramway from the point where it crosses the Haytor/Manaton road, westward to the Holwell Tor quarry, ignoring all left hand branches. After about a mile you will find the line going downhill quite quickly. At the bottom of this incline are the Holwell quarry faces on the left of the tramway, just past the ruined building, also on the left. Just beyond the quarry face, on the other side of the tramway, a steep incline leads down to a little plateau about ten feet below the level of the tramway—and there is the shelter, a feature I believe to be unique in Dartmoor industrial archaeology.

NOTES TO THIS CHAPTER.

Much more information about the Haytor quarries and tramway and the other quarries mentioned can be found in:
The Haytor Granite Tramway and Stover Canal, by M. C. Ewans. Published by David & Charles, Newton Abbot, 1964 (this is still in print).
Industrial Archaeology of Dartmoor, by Helen Harris. Published by David & Charles, Newton Abbot, 1964. (Also in print.)
Excursions embracing the Haytor quarries and tramway and the Foggin Tor, Swell Tor and King Tor quarries are included in *Exploring Dartmoor* by F. H. Starkey. Published by the author at Haytor Vale, 1980. (Also in print.)

6

BELSTONE

The little village of Belstone occupies a position on the extreme northern edge of Dartmoor and possesses to my mind almost everything that a moorland village should have. Some of these attributes will be dealt with shortly, but first let us consider the matter of approach. Belstone lies to the south of the A.30 trunk road and is approached from that road by no less than four lanes. One of these, the westernmost one, is signposted by the highway authority "Belstone— indirect", a kind thought for the benefit of the wayfarer who might otherwise think that he had somehow lost his way, so serpentine is the road. My own favourite approach however is by way of the lane that leaves the A.30 just west of Sticklepath. This is signposted "Skaigh" and the fact that you can get to Belstone that way is a deep dark secret. But you can, and with no great difficulty, although the road is narrow, steep and winding in places, but so beautiful, especially at the northern end, that it is all well worth while. At one spot along this road, near one of the bends, crumbling masonry will be seen on either side of the road and there is a steep drop on the left of the road. Find somewhere convenient to park and approach on foot and you will discover the remains of ruined buildings and much running water. These ruins are those of the Taw River Copper Mine and among them can be detected the wheel pit in which revolved the largest water-wheel ever to be erected in England. This was installed in 1878/79 and its purpose was to work the pumps which drained the workings of the mine. The wheel was 70 feet in diameter, only $2\frac{1}{2}$ feet smaller than the largest ever built in the United Kingdom. This was at Laxey in the Isle of Man and was $72\frac{1}{2}$ feet in diameter. It is said that the Belstone wheel was painted bright red and so startling was the sight of this great wheel revolving and so tremendous the noise it made that horses drawing vehicles along the road could not be persuaded to pass the wheel.

About three-quarters of a mile further on the road runs into Belstone village, meeting another road coming from the north near the village green. And now we can begin to savour the true delights of this charming backwater. On the edge of the green stand the village stocks, in good working order and complete with a great block of granite for the detainee to sit upon; comfort was not the most important part of the punishment one imagines. Nearby is the pound, a tiny circular enclosure in which stray cattle were imprisoned until claimed—and ransomed—by their owner. Next door is the pound-keeper's cottage, aptly named "Pound Cottage". Also on the green is a lamp-post, mounted upon a tall granite column. This was erected to commemorate the Coronation of King George V. At the green the road divides. Take the one on the left and it will deliver you onto the grassy slopes below which the River Taw flows through Belstone Cleave. The road itself ends a quarter of a mile from the village at a place called Birchy Lake; beyond this is the open moor. The road to the right of the green takes the explorer past the Post Office, church and pub and continuing for a third of a mile or so ends at the moorgate on Watchet Hill. Beyond the gate—kept closed please because of wandering stock—lies the vast expanse of Dartmoor. From this spot to the southernmost point on Dartmoor, near Ivybridge, is about 23 miles; a fair day's walk as many hardy Dartmoorians prove every year.

In his great book *"Devon"*, which came out in 1954, Professor W. G. Hoskins speaks somewhat slightingly of some atrocious modern buildings erected in Belstone early this century and waxes indignant about what was done to the church when it was restored in 1881. One has to agree with these comments, but a careful look at village and church will reveal much of interest and beauty. For example, the Post Office. This is still labelled "Telegraph Office" and has a distinctly ecclesiastical look about it. Close examination brings to light a carved stone which proves that the building was once a dissenting chapel, and the mystery is solved. The pub is the Tors Hotel and is almost certainly one of the buildings which annoyed Professor Hoskins. I must agree that the building itself does nothing for me, but the welcome is warm and the fare is good—one can demand little more of any pub. And there are still, in the centre of the village and scattered around the area, a number of truly beautiful farmhouses and cottages of the type which make Devon famous for its vernacular buildings.

One of the features Belstone lacks is a village cross. This thought occurred to me many years ago when my interest in these matters was

The Telegraph Office, Belstone.

Stone coffin lid? Belstone churchyard.

first being aroused and it is interesting to note that a much earlier visitor had the same thought. Writing in 1862 an anonymous contributor to *"The Gentleman's Magazine"* recounts how he visited Belstone, noted that the stocks were there then, as now, and noted too that there appeared to be no village cross and enquired for it. He was told that the cross used to stand attached to an old house near the church. When the house was pulled down, several years before, the Rector purchased the materials and removed the cross to his private garden. The enquirer did not pursue his search any further so we do not know what he would have found at the rectory. William Crossing seems to have been told the same story when making enquiries at Belstone later in the 19th century. He failed to find the cross but did discover, in the lane leading to the old Belstone Rectory, a stone inscribed with a cross which could have been the source of the rather garbled story just related.

Many years ago the stone referred to above was moved to the churchyard at Belstone and this is where we can now find it, leaning against the wall of the tower. This is a slab of granite inscribed with a cross within a circle. Below the cross is a segment of another circle which is bisected by a perpendicular line. The stone is a little over four feet long and varies in width from 12 to 18 inches. This can never have been a village cross; it was probably part of the lid of a stone coffin or sarcophagus. There are one or two other fragments of worked stone lying near the one just described; they are almost certainly pieces of broken tombstones.

St Mary's Church, Belstone, is a typical Dartmoor church with a low squat tower of 15th century type. As one would expect, the whole building is of granite and although plain it is, to me at least, beautiful in its simplicity. As Professor Hoskins says, the church was drastically restored in 1881, and it may be, as he says, that everything of interest so far as the interior was concerned was swept away at that time. But it is easy to be critical at a century's distance and we ought not to be too severe unless we are sure we know just what the restorers had to contend with. I possess a little book *"Belstone"*, written in 1911 by Miss D. James, who I understand to have been the daughter of a former Rector of Belstone. The author's account of the history of Belstone and its church is a fascinating one and obviously cannot be reproduced here. But she has much to say about the condition of the church in the 19th century, taken from contemporary records and they reveal an appalling state of affairs, for example:

1871: The entrance porch is very dirty, poultry having been allowed to get in. Unless the Church is restored it must fall.

1871: Two or three panes of glass are broken in the East window. The flooring is very damp. . . . The bell frames are in very bad repair. . . . The South aisle roof is bad. . . . and the ceiling falling in. . . . The Church is damp.

1873: The books are much torn and the Bible imperfect. . . .

1874: The bells were re-hung, the ropes having become so rotten that to ring any bell a man had to climb up into the tower and sound it like a gong.

1881: . . . a greater part of the roof leaked badly and in the south aisle it was actually falling in . . . the flooring in the pews was in many places unsafe and . . . apt to give way in a very alarming fashion.

In 1881, at long last, a wholesale restoration of the church was undertaken at a cost of £800, a very large sum in those days. But the neglect had been so prolonged and complete that much of the woodwork was beyond repair. It was found necessary to remove the oak screen, the whole of the pews and the gallery at the end of the South aisle. This gallery used to accommodate the orchestra, apparently there was no organ, and the choir. The instruments consisted of a violin, a violoncello, a bass viol and a flute. The violin and the 'cello were both still in active use when Miss James wrote her book in 1911. The tale of woe related above surely explains why the restoration was not as satisfactory as might have been desirable. To a poor and thinly populated parish the task of finding the money for such an expensive and exhaustive operation must have been almost overwhelming. At least we are left with a plain but beautiful little church which sits in its setting as though it were made for it—as indeed it was.

But Belstone does not consist merely of the village, interesting though that is. The parish of Belstone extends southwards from the village for considerably more than a mile in places, embracing all the open moorland between the valley of the East Okement on the west and the Taw on the east.

The southern extremity of the parish cuts across the common from Cullever Steps on the East Okement to a point on the Taw opposite the summit of Cosdon Hill. The line of this boundary has been the subject of much dispute in the past, as the profusion of boundary stones on the ground and contradictory boundary lines on maps and elsewhere serve to show. South of the Belstone boundary the Forest of Dartmoor extends for more than fifteen miles to Broad Rock beyond the valley of the Plym. Bisecting the boundary is the magnificent ridge of the Belstone Tors, or rather three Belstone Tors, and Higher Tor, Winter Tor, Knattborough Tor and southernmost of all, Oke Tor, overlooking Steeperton Gorge. This splendid range, one of northern Dartmoor's principal features, is straddled by the enigmatic Irishman's Wall. There is also a profusion of prehistoric monuments, one of which, the Nine Maidens, consists of a circle of 16 stones, some erect some fallen, which are said to revolve at noon each day, thus continuing the ancient tradition that the stones were originally young girls who were turned to stone as a punishment for dancing on the Sabbath. The hillside below the tors has been the scene of much surface quarrying in times past and signs of this activity are everywhere to be seen, including partly made and abandoned artifacts such as apple-crushers, troughs, gate-posts and the like.

Finally, a short rhyme illustrating the Belstone tradition that when attending church in the old days men and women separated and sat on opposite sides of the church—men on the south and women on the north side.

"The churches and chapels, we usually find,
Are the places where men unto women are join'd;
But at Belstone it seems, they are more cruel hearted,
For men and their women are brought here to be parted."

7

FIASCOS

In English the word fiasco has come to mean an unexpected and inexplicable breakdown or failure in a performance or project. But we had the word from the French who in turn adopted it from the Italian language and in that language its original meaning was "a flask or bottle". Only in modern times have the Italians given it the meaning it bears in English and there it still retains its original meaning also. How did all this come about? The dictionaries are vague on the point and usually content themselves with the comment "an unexplained allusion", or some such remark. I have no personal knowledge of this matter but I very well remember, in the days of my youth, a much respected tutor making a suggestion which seemed to me then to satisfactorily explain the matter, and still does. The master in question was one who found the freaks and vagaries of language as fascinating as I do now. He suggested that the connotation—fiasco— flask—failure may have sprung from an incident common in the glassblower's experience, when a partly made flask or bottle suddenly collapsed under the blowpipe for no apparent reason. So that fiasco = flask and flask = failure, leaving us where we are today. If you want to know what all this has to do with Dartmoor now read on.

The Dartmoor explorer who has learned to use his eyes will find that he constantly comes across signs of human activity throughout the length and breadth of the Moor. Sometimes these signs will be the ruined dwellings, ritual monuments and other erections left behind by the prehistoric inhabitants of the region. Other traces will consist of the remains of buildings, both industrial and residential, and boundary walls and other features abandoned by the early Saxon settlers and the medieval farmers, tin-miners and others who lived upon and exploited the Moor for their own benefit.

Apart from the boundary banks (known on Dartmoor as reaves) of varying age and the great pits and gullies created by the tinners, almost everything that man has left behind him on Dartmoor is made from solid stone, usually granite or "moorstone" as the surface granite is called. Buildings, from 2000 BC to the 19th century AD, walls, gateposts, direction signs, boundary stones, wayside crosses, cattle troughs, hand-mills, millstones, apple-crushers, mortars on which to crush tin-ore, tinners' moulds, chutes to direct swill into the pig-trough and a hundred other uses were found for the ubiquitous granite. Bearing all this in mind and remembering that granite is a somewhat intractable rock, not easy to work, especially with primitive tools and liable to contain hidden flaws, it is not surprising that many failures were experienced and that many granite fiascos are to be found lying on the surface of the Moor. The granite region of Dartmoor covers some 250 square miles and it is therefore not to be wondered at that no complete catalogue of these abandoned items has ever been compiled, or is ever likely to be. After more than thirty years of exploring Dartmoor it is still the case that I seldom end a day's excursion without having found some new—new to me that is—feature to add to the list. Recent such discoveries include a granite trough, nearly finished but split from end to end as the final touches were applied; an agricultural roller, about six feet long, not yet

Broken trough, Smallacombe Rocks, Haytor.

cylindrical but approaching that form and the stem of a staddle stone, beautifully formed but with the narrow end broken off.

Who was responsible for all this work and all these heartbreaking failures? The answer has to be that generally speaking they were the work of the men who worked the farms in the vicinity and whose tenancies gave them rights of common. These included not only the right to pasture animals on the commons, but also the privilege of taking from the Moor "anything that might do them good, saving only green oak and venison". The passage just quoted applied in particular to the tenants of the Duchy of Cornwall in and around the Forest of Dartmoor, but the rights of other commoners were much the same. It is known that rights of common have existed on Dartmoor from at least the 13th century and probably for very much longer. And as they still exist today, though they are not perhaps exercised to the same extent as formerly, it is not surprising that so many relics of past practices still exist.

8

WHEAL BETSY

The Dartmoor landscape and its immediate margins are littered from end to end with relics of ancient mining enterprises—mine dumps, spoil heaps, trial pits, opencast workings, shafts—open and sealed, adits and leats, and above all buildings, buildings of all ages from as early perhaps as the 15th century to a few of the 20th. In the interior of the Moor, along the banks of rivers and streams, are the ruins of many ancient buildings associated with the tin mining industry which formerly flourished here. Many of these buildings, where tin ore was crushed, separated and smelted between the 12th and 18th centuries, are shown on the Ordnance Survey maps as "blowing houses". Today the tendency is to call them tinners' mills, because it is now realised that they were not merely smelting houses but fulfilled other functions connected with the preparation of the ore.

Around the perimeter of the Moor other minerals besides tin were mined and smelted. These included copper, arsenic, bismuth, manganese, zinc, lead and silver, and iron ore of different kinds. The buildings and other relics of these latter activities are often more easily discernable than those of the tin mining industry, because whilst tinning had largely ceased, except here and there, by the middle of the 19th century, the mining of other metals went on until well into the present century.

One of the most spectacular ruins associated with the later phase of mining on Dartmoor is to be found beside the A.386 road (Tavistock to Okehampton) east of the road about a mile north of the village of Mary Tavy. This is the shell and chimney stack of the engine house of Wheal Betsy mine. Wheal Betsy produced not only silver and lead but also in its time copper and arsenic. Obviously of great age it was reopened in 1806. The machinery of the mine, pumps, winding gear and so on, was worked by water power until 1868. Then the building we see today was built to house a Cornish beam pumping engine worked by steam, the fuel for which was largely peat brought from the remote Walkham Head peat diggings on northern Dartmoor. From then until the mine finally closed down in 1877 all the pumping, winding and ore crushing was done by steam power. When the mine ceased work the machinery was removed and sold off and the buildings were abandoned. When I first saw Wheal Betsy in the 1950's more than seventy years of neglect had taken its toll and the building was then a gaunt and crumbling ruin, both roof and floors having fallen in. But despite its apparently parlous condition the structure of this fine old building was still sound and in 1967 it was acquired and made safe by the National Trust "as a memorial to the Mining Industry of Dartmoor".

One of the reasons for preserving the engine house of Wheal Betsy must have been the fact that it is unique in the industrial archaeology of Dartmoor. In Cornwall such buildings are quite common; indeed, here and there specimens have been acquired by the National Trust and put back into working order for the pleasure and information of people who are interested in such matters. But on Dartmoor the situation is far different. In fact Wheal Betsy is the only specimen left to us, if indeed others ever did exist. I know of no firm evidence that

Wheal Betsy, general view down the valley.

DTN-D

this was so but it has been suggested that there was a similar building at Ringleshutts Mine, on Holne Moor. But so little is known of the history of that mine and the buildings that remain are so ruinous that it is almost impossible to be sure what they were.

One final item of interest about Wheal Betsy, though this may be more in the nature of folk-lore than historical fact. The chimney stack of the old building must be something over forty feet in height and, seen from some angles, it is clearly well out of the perpendicular: there is a distinct curve in the upper half. And yet the structure is obviously quite sound. Twenty-five or more years ago, whilst on holiday from London, I found myself one lunch-time in the Peter Tavy Inn and fell into conversation with an elderly native. He, like most Devonians, was delighted to talk to someone who was obviously interested in Dartmoor and among other things I told him of my visit to Wheal Betsy that morning and commented about the crooked chimney. "Ah! yes", said my friend, "you know how that happened don't you?" He then went on to tell me that "years ago" when the chimney was under construction the builders were a certain local mason and his mate. Apparently their plan of action was that each had a spell of laying the granite blocks whilst the other acted as his labourer; then they changed over for a spell, and so on. One day the mason was ill and could not come to work but so as not to hold up the job his mate decided to continue on his own. He obviously found the task rather more than he had reckoned on, not only having to lay the blocks but also carry up the stone and mortar, adjust the scaffolding when necessary and everything else the job entailed. The result was that when the mason came back to work after a week or so the chimney was nearly complete. But when the scaffolding was removed the very noticeable kink in the shaft was revealed for all to see, much to the dismay of the builder and his mate. "But", said my informant, "you can only see the bend from some angles and as 'er looked all right otherwise they decided to leave 'er be. And 'er still be all right, bain't she?" The answer of course is "Yes, she be". Go and see for yourself, access is easy and free. But be careful where you park your car and watch the children who may be tempted to clamber about on the rather rough hillside.

9

SIDELIGHTS ON THE MILITARY OCCUPATION OF DARTMOOR

The newly fledged Dartmoor lover will find, very early in his explorations, that his activities in some parts of the Moor are considerably hampered by the presence of the Armed Forces of the Crown. This is particularly true on northern Dartmoor where firing with live ammunition takes place, within the boundaries of the National Park, sometimes as frequently as four days a week. For military purposes the Moor is divided into three Ranges known as the Okehampton, Merivale and Willsworthy Ranges. Military activities also take place over a wide area south of Princetown known as the Cramber Tor Area but here no live firing takes place. On the days when live firing is scheduled on the three main ranges the public are excluded from the area concerned. It not infrequently happens that firing takes place on all three ranges simultaneously, with the result that on those occasions something like 60 square miles, or getting on for 40,000 acres are prohibited for public access.

The boundaries of the ranges are marked by lines of red and white poles. There are also large numbers of warning notice boards on and around the ranges and red flags (or at night red lights) are displayed on firing days from prominent places around the perimeter of the ranges affected. The firing programme for the ensuing nine days is published weekly in *The Western Morning News* and is also displayed in post offices around the Moor.

From the foregoing it will be apparent that anyone planning an excursion to the north or north-western areas of Dartmoor is well advised to find out what firing is scheduled for that day. Generally speaking no firing takes place on Dartmoor during the month of August or on Sundays.

It is not the purpose of this chapter to inveigh against the military and governmental policies which permit the use of a National Park for live firing or indeed any kind of firing by the armed forces. That still un-won battle has been raging for more than a century with governments of both Left and Right on the one side and the Dartmoor Preservation Association, the Ramblers' Association and many other amenity bodies on the other. My own standpoint is simply stated. I cannot understand how anyone, even a politician, can hope to reconcile the idea of a National Park, established with the purpose of caring for and making accessible to the public an area of outstanding natural beauty with the use of that same area for battle training with live ammunition and explosives. The thing is a ridiculous anomaly; it has already lasted a hundred years too long and the sooner it ceases altogether the better.

Having said all that however it is nevertheless the truth that military activities on Dartmoor have left behind them some interesting remains which are bound to arouse the interest and curiosity of the explorer who comes across them. Many of these features have now been abandoned for so long that they have become, or are becoming, military antiquities in their own right and so worthy of study, or at least of notice. I have no intention of compiling a list of the objects in question, my knowledge is too incomplete for that. Suffice it to say that I seldom spend a day in the vicinity of the ranges on Dartmoor without having come across some previously unknown (to me) specimen.

Most of the items of military archaeology referred to above will be found on the northern moor, within a comparatively short distance of the battle camp at Okehampton. For examples: the target railway near the headwaters of the Moor Brook on the eastern slopes of West Mill Tor and a similar though less interesting one about a mile away to the west, on Black Down. These railways were used to provide a moving target for the gunners; the one near West Mill Tor describes a complete loop and is equipped with an enginehouse in which, I am told, the motor driven locomotive is still housed. Military remains of a somewhat older vintage, perhaps Victorian or Edwardian, will be

Rowtor (Okehampton) and rifle butts.

Part of target railway and engine house, below West Mill Tor.

found on the riverside plain on the left bank of the River Taw downstream from Steeperton Gorge. These consist of a series of small stonebuilt U shaped rifle-butts, clearly of a later date than the tinners' heaps and remains among which they stand.

Another item of the same genus has now become the object of interest and enquiries, although only abandoned in the 1960's or 70's.

This is the site and equipment of the former Rippon Tor rifle range. These are close by the roadside on Mountsland Common, about two miles north of Ashburton. The remains consist of four immense grass covered mounds and a tremendous cliff of concrete in front of which stands the machinery, still largely complete, for raising and lowering the targets.

When this range was in use Rippon Tor itself, a mile and a half to the north, was in the danger area and public access was forbidden when firing was taking place, so perhaps some progress has been made. I used to think that this installation was an unsightly eyesore and had I been asked ten years ago I would unhesitatingly have recommended that it be removed lock, stock and barrel. But today I am not so sure. Quite apart from the fact that it would cost a fortune to remove it I have come to think that perhaps the remains may be of considerable interest to future generations. What a pity it would have been for example, and how much less interesting Dartmoor would be today, if the old tinners had removed all their buildings and filled in all their workings; and how much less we would have known about their activities. So perhaps we should just tidy up the site and leave it alone to mellow?

A final item to whet the appetite, though there are many more for the observant explorer to find. A mile to the south-west of Princetown and just north of Hart Tor is the site of a Victorian rifle range. The target butts are at the foot of the tor and the range is marked by a number (I seem to remember eight) of finely worked granite posts, each inscribed with its distance in yards from the target—50, 100 and so on. I think this range has to be a survivor from the middle of the 19th century when the convict prison was first established and soldiers were employed to guard the prisoners because no Prison Service yet existed. But here I am guessing.

Very early in his wanderings on the Dartmoor ranges the explorer will begin to find other signs of the military occupation of the Moor— signs other than buildings I mean. For example, here and there a roughly cuboid structure of brick or concrete will be found. These are about 2 feet in each dimension and sometimes they are fitted with a door, sometimes not. These structures are field telephone points, frequently long disused, but apparently never removed when redundant. Often associated with these latter items lengths of once buried telephone cables will be seen peeping from the ground. Vehicle tracks, splinter-proof shelters, range and notice boards and shell and mortar craters are everywhere; an extraordinary variety of military litter is unbelievably widespread. The latter category includes such items as brass cartridge cases (rifle ammunition), either blanks or spent; fragments of metal shell cases of varying sizes, some with the brass driving band still in position; mortar bombs and flares of various kinds are commonplace. Some of the items found are clearly of great age and it is apparent that most are harmless, having exploded on impact. But now and again one finds something that could be dangerous and then there is only one safe rule to obey—leave severely alone anything that could conceivably be unexploded. This particularly applies to mortar bombs which are sometimes found sticking out of the ground, complete with fins, in a very sinister manner. Anything of this kind should be reported to the police or the military authorities. Over the years we have found large numbers of small lead balls, sometimes just lying on the surface of the ground, sometimes on the edge of a track or crater. These vary in size, but on average would be about half an inch in diameter. At first we thought that these might be leaden musket balls of an earlier generation, but later, having found them in numbers and associated with shards of shell cases, we came to the conclusion that they were probably caseshot, i.e. the non-explosive missiles contained in a shrapnel shell. Again, not being military historians, this is no more than a guess.

Quite apart from the appalling thought that dangerous explosives may be lying about in a National Park the fact that so much litter is engendered by the military presence is quite unacceptable. To be fair it should be said that things are not as bad as they were a few years ago, but considerable deposits are still to be found, including caches of tin cans and other containers clearly of military origin.

NOTES

A very concise and readable account of the history of military activities on Dartmoor will be found in *Dartmoor—a New Study*, edited by Crispin Gill, especially Chapter 9 by John Somers Cocks. Published by David & Charles. Also, if you can find copies, in the Reference Library perhaps, two pamphlets issued by the Dartmoor Preservation Association and the Standing Committee on National Parks in 1964 and 1965 respectively:

Misuse of a National Park—Military Training on Dartmoor (DPA).
and
National Land Use and the Dartmoor National Park (SCNP).

This chapter first appeared, in a slightly different form, in the *Dartmoor Magazine* in 1985. I am indebted to the Editors of that publication for their permission to use it here.

10

THE RUGGLESTONE

Over the years I suppose dozens of people have asked me, in varying terms but essentially the same question: "I noticed something on the map, near Widecombe, called the Rugglestone. What is it?" The answer to this is simple, i.e. that the Rugglestone is a tiny tor two of the sections of which are, or were, loganstones. What is a logan stone? It is a natural rock of considerable size and weight which is so finely balanced that it can be made to rock or "log" by the exertion of pressure by human weight or strength. It used to be thought that these stones were a device of the Druids with which they impressed their congregations; it is now known that they are purely natural features produced by the forces of wind and weather acting upon the structure of the rock. There are scores of these rocking stones on Dartmoor, many of them marked upon the maps, many not. Several of those identified by previous generations have now lost their logging qualities but no doubt others are being formed by the forces of nature and new ones frequently come to light.

The Rugglestone, one of Dartmoor's most famous logan stones, lies on the edge of the common at the foot of Widecombe Hill, less than half a mile from the church. It can best be approached from the road which runs from Widecombe village to the hamlet of Venton from where a footpath extends to the rock. The Rugglestone is approachable with ease only during a dry period; at other times the ground around it is very wet. On arrival the visitor will find a granite mass composed of large slabs superimposed one upon the other. Two of these slabs are said to have had rocking qualities in the past. The larger one, computed to weigh about 115 tons, could, it is said, only be moved with the assistance of the church door key. According to William Crossing the latter stone could be made to log slightly in his day. Personally I have never been able to shift either of them.

The Rugglestone, Widecombe in the Moor.

Pretty well all the older Dartmoor writers mention the Rugglestone, but apart from commenting upon the rocking qualities it then possessed and the immense weight of the larger stone none has anything to say about any historical or social significance the rock may have had. However it has always seemed to me that for some reason, as yet unidentified, the Rugglestone occupied a special place in the minds of local people and hence in the writings of the older topographers, though it is only fair to comment that nearly all these same writers also mention the famous Nutcracker Rock on Rippon Tor. This too was a logan in times past; it was destroyed by vandals in 1975. On many occasions during the last thirty years or so I have enquired of local people whether they had any knowledge of any ancient tradition or tale associated with the Rugglestone. These enquiries have been almost totally unproductive; on one occasion only I got the reply "Oh, I believe that was where the villagers used to meet when they wanted to talk privately". And that was all, my informant either knew no more or was prepared to say no more; I was after all, a stranger. There is however what may be one tiny ray of light upon this subject. In his splendid novel of Dartmoor life *"Widecombe Fair"* Eden

45

Phillpotts places the action of one whole chapter at and in the vicinity of the Rugglestone. The novel was published in 1912 and the action takes place at Widecombe in the Moor around the turn of the 19th/20th centuries. It is a very crowded stage that the author presents to his audience, but among the characters portrayed are the weak and nervous landlord of the Old Inn, his buxom, overbearing and passionate wife and her would-be lover, the village blacksmith. As the momentum of her liaison with the blacksmith intensifies the lady takes to bullying her unfortunate husband, even going so far as to strike him in public on occasions. The villagers greatly resent the scandalous goings on and particularly the treatment of her husband by the erring wife and it is decided to teach her a lesson—the woman always pays. The punishment is to take the form of a public showing-up which is to consist of a mock trial, execution and burial of an effigy of the offending woman. This takes place at the Rugglestone where most of the population of the village are assembled, either in support of the demonstration or to oppose it. The trial takes place, and then the execution, preceded by the singing of a dirge;

> "There is a wife lives in this place
> Who beats her husband to sad disgrace.
> She beats him black, and she beats him blue,
> She beats him till the blood runs through!
> And if this woman don't mend her manners,
> We'll have her skin and send to the tanners;
> And when the tanners have tanned it well,
> Her hide shall be hung on the nail of hell!"

After the execution—hanging on the gallows of course—the burial was begun, the grave having been dug in advance. But now the opposition showed its teeth and battle was engaged. Several people suffered more or less minor injuries and as darkness fell the crowd drifted away to the pubs or the doctor's or to lick their wounds or talk over the events of the evening. But was this episode pure author's invention or did the author come across some piece of Widecombe history that I so far have failed to uncover? I wish I knew.

11

DARTMOOR SCHOOLS

While laying down the foundations for this chapter I came across an item of information which led me to read up the history of education in much greater depth than had been my original intention. The spur which impelled me to this unusual cerebral activity was a passage that told me, to my astonishment, that in India, two thousand years ago, universities existed at which such subjects as theology, medicine, law, astronomy and art were taught. There were six of these universities which were open only to male members of the Brahman caste. Such a university would probably have had a hundred lecture rooms and ten thousand students; the course lasted 12 years. Immediately before reading the passage from which I culled the above items of information I had been re-reading—for the umpteenth time—William Crossing's *"One Hundred Years on Dartmoor"* in which he draws a picture of life on the Moor during the 19th century. Among many other topics Crossing briefly touches upon the education available to Dartmoor children during the century in question. He says, *inter alia*, "In most of the border villages a dame's school, or that of a rustic pedagogue might be found, and some of the children, more favoured than others, were taught to read and perhaps to write. But this was by no means general, while those whose homes were at all remote never received any instruction whatever".

We know that educational facilities in Devon villages improved considerably from the 1830's onward with the coming of the first parliamentary grants towards public education, and the establishment of the first National Schools; this of course was true of the Dartmoor border villages as elsewhere. But it is clear that the conditions described by Crossing continued for many years as far as children living on remote Dartmoor farms were concerned. In fact it was not until 1876 that active steps were taken to provide reasonable schooling for these children. In that year the chapels of St. Raphael at Huccaby and St. Gabriel at Postbridge were built, the intention being to provide chapels of ease for those members of the Anglican faith who otherwise had no church of their sect available to them nearer than, for examples, the parish churches at Widecombe and Lydford. But the erection of these chapels also had the effect of providing suitable buildings for use as schools, and for many years the two chapels doubled as places of worship on Sundays and as schools on weekdays. Huccaby chapel, known as Dartmeet School, opened in 1878 and closed in 1925. Postbridge chapel opened as a school in 1879 and survived until 1931. These schools were managed by a committee with the rector of Lydford as chairman. At the same time the National School provided for the families of prison staff at Princetown was made available to other children living within the Forest of Dartmoor.

It was a recent visit to St. Raphael's Chapel at Huccaby that gave me the idea of including a chapter on Dartmoor schools in this book. St. Raphael's, like its sister chapel at Postbridge, is a delightful little granite church. It is nearly always unlocked and is well worth a visit to anyone interested in such matters. I was surprised and very pleased to find that the old school desks and forms, complete with holes for inkwells, and other items of school paraphernalia were still in position. There is also a massive granite fireplace. The chapel is of course still a place of worship in regular use. My visit to St. Raphael's made a profound impression on me and I was easily able to reconstruct the sights and sounds that must have taken place here and to remind myself that more than sixty years ago I was a pupil at a very similar school in Yorkshire. There were about 35 of us pupils, of all ages between 5 and 14 and we shared the attentions of our one teacher, Miss Briggs, a middle aged dragon with the voice of a sergeant-major and a heart of pure gold.

There is a very strong tradition in the vicinity of Huccaby and Hexworthy that the school at Huccaby chapel was preceded by an earlier one, not far away. I know of no written confirmation of this but since the tradition is specific in its details and the site still available it seems worth mentioning. About a mile to the north-west of the junction where the B.3357 road meets the Hexworthy road, just west of Dartmeet, a little stream passes under the road. The stream is the Cocks Lake which rises a short distance to the north in Brimpts

The Schoolhouse, Cocks Lake, Huccaby.

49

Newtake. Quite near the road a pattern of little fields lies on either side of the stream. Associated with these is a ruined and abandoned farmstead also known as Cocks Lake. The main building here has clearly been at least partially rebuilt at some time and it is known locally as School House. This is the site, so it is said, of the former school. What a lonely isolated place for a school you will think. And so it is—the nearest houses, Huccaby Cottage and Dunnabridge Pound Farm, are both more than half a mile away to the south-east and south-west respectively. Education did not come easily to the children of Dartmoor a century and more ago.

There are many other remains and sites of Dartmoor schools around the Moor for those who care to seek them out. A few examples of some of those I find most interesting are given below.

The village of Ilsington stands on the south-eastern edge of Dartmoor, next door to Widecombe in fact. Ilsington parish is immense and has within its bounds extensive commons, including Haytor Down, site of the once famous Haytor Granite Quarries. Just to the east of the long disused quarries, nearly two miles from Ilsington village, will be found a spot surrounded by low stone walls and traversed by the Haytor Granite Tramway. This is the site of the original Haytor village, a collection of houses and other buildings erected to serve the quarry labour force in the 1820's. Tradition has it that the village had not only houses but a pub as well and that another building existed which was used as a school during the week and as a chapel on Sunday. I have a copy of an old print, made in 1829, which gives a good view of the village, including the school-cum-chapel which was equipped with a bell to call the faithful to worship and the scholars to school, according to the day of the week.

In Ilsington village itself stands the parish church of St. Michael. The main entrance to the churchyard is by way of the lychgate and over the gate is an arch formed by the floor of the parish room which is above. Access to the parish room is by means of a narrow granite stairway. In former days the room over the lychgate was used as the village school, a very early one, for in 1639 there took place here an event which has become quite famous in Devon history. The occurrence is fully documented in the Church Register, under date Sept. 17th 1639, which can best be paraphrased as follows. On the day in question there were present in the schoolroom the schoolmaster, Mr. H. Corbin and 17 of his scholars, all boys. Twelve other pupils

The Parish Room, St. Michael's Church, Ilsington.

were absent from school that day. At about 11am a woman entered the churchyard via the lychgate and in passing through let the heavy gate fall to behind her. She had gone only a few feet when the south wall of the schoolroom collapsed, allowing the roof to do likewise. The roof brought down the other walls so that, in the words of the record, ". . . not one stick, stone or pin of the whole structure remayning where it was formerly placed. . . ." The record goes on to relate that four of the pupils fell down into the churchyard and escaped with little injury. Others were struck by timbers and stones and one was trapped in the room beneath the debris. Another was flung out into the street and then covered with debris so that nothing of him could be seen. But eventually he was dug out and was found, like all the others, to have suffered no serious injury. The record concludes: "At the wrighting hereof they are all in health and soe living to Praise God for their deliverance."

51

About two miles south of Chagford is a very ancient farm called Yeo. Some parts of the existing buildings may well be of 13th century date, or earlier. In fact there is little doubt that Yeo was an early Saxon settlement. On a recent visit to Yeo we were shown these ancient buildings by the farmer, Mr Loram, whose wife's family have farmed here for centuries. One of the outbuildings was clearly once a dwelling, being equipped with a great stone fireplace and other indications of human occupation. Mr Loram told us that this building was formerly a Dame School, such as those referred to by Crossing, where local children came to be taught to read by the dame or male teacher, whose reward was the few pence a week paid by the parents of their pupils. Few of these teachers had any qualifications as such and many of them had other occupations which they carried on simultaneously with their teaching activities. The standard of instruction was very low; usually the only reading material available was the Bible and so the reading lesson qualified as religious instruction as well. At many of these schools no attempt was made to teach the children to write, this being a skill not regarded as necessary or even desirable for the working classes of the day, it might have given them ideas above their station!

There were scores of Dame schools in Devon in the 18th century and many lingered on in very remote areas until the end of the 19th century. Dartmoor had several of these schools and one in particular comes to mind as having had a somewhat odd reputation. This was at Rundlestone, about a mile from Princetown, on the Tavistock road. There are still some very primitive cottages at Rundlestone, not now occupied as dwellings, and one of these may have housed the school. The story goes that during a "reading aloud" lesson it would often happen that the child reached a word which was unfamiliar or which the pupil could not pronounce, and so stopped. When this happened the teacher would say, "Never mind, say 'possible' and read on." And the lesson continued. Thus the flow of activity was maintained and lengthy interruptions while explanations were given were avoided. Remembering some of the personal and place names in the Old Testament one realises that the situation described must often have arisen.

About half a mile west of Rundlestone a Water Authority pump-house will be seen on the right, close to the road. A few yards further on, on the common but near the road, will be found the outline of a small rectangular building. This was the site of the Fogginer Mission

Hall, which stood here until the 1960's, when it was demolished. For many years the Mission Hall did duty as a school for the children of the quarrymen who worked at the Foggintor, Swell Tor and King Tor quarries nearby. These were the children of the thirty or more families who lived in the adjacent Red Cottages and those at Foggintor itself, all now demolished. The use of the Mission Hall as a school continued until 1913 when a purpose-built school was erected at Four Winds, about half a mile further west and on the other side of the road. This was officially known as Walkhampton Foggintor School and remained in use until 1936 when it closed down. The few remaining pupils were transferred to Princetown. I first remember seeing this building as a windowless and weatherbeaten shell in the early 1950's. It was demolished in 1965 and the site is now a very useful car-park. But one can still see where the school stood and the outline of the playgrounds, surrounded as they are by granite walls.

At Foggintor Quarry too there is a strong tradition of an earlier school and a number of local people have spoken to me about it. Indeed, getting on for twenty years ago we were taken to the site by a very elderly lady who told us that her mother had been a teacher here and who identified the ruined building which she thought she remembered as the school. I am not sure about this identification but I do feel sure that there was a school quite close to the quarry in the 19th century. The quarry has of course been long abandoned but some of the ruined buildings are quite spectacular in appearance. But be warned, they are crumbling rapidly and likely to be dangerous to people who clamber about on the ruins.

The above does not pretend to be a catalogue of former Dartmoor schools, but merely a few specimens of what is there to be found by the interested explorer. Almost every parish around the Moor has some old school building or site to show, some of them several and all with an interesting history. Just one more facet of the enormous range of interests that Dartmoor has to offer.

FURTHER READING

Devon Village Schools in the nineteenth century, by Roger. R. Sellman, one time Devon County Council Inspector of Schools. Published by David & Charles, Newton Abbot (1967). Also: An article, *Memories of a School on the Moor,* by Barbara Stevens in the *Western Morning News,* 22nd December, 1984. (This is the Foggintor School, mentioned above.)

DTN-E

12

BURNARD'S "DARTMOOR PICTORIAL RECORDS"

Some few years ago I was fortunate enough to come into possession of the four volumes of Robert Burnard's *"Dartmoor Pictorial Records"*. This rare work was privately published in four parts between 1890 and 1894 at the rate of roughly one volume per year—there was none in 1892. Only 150 copies of Volume I were ever printed and only 200 copies of each of the other three. Each copy of each volume is dated and numbered and signed by the author and by the printer, W. Brendon of Plymouth.

In view of the very abbreviated print-runs it is not surprising that few complete sets of the four volumes have survived. The books were originally quarter-bound in calf but unfortunately the leather chosen was not of lasting quality, with the result that many of the surviving volumes are in poor condition. My own set had to be completely re-bound before I dare subject them to normal wear and tear. However, the paper and printing are of superb quality and apart from a little discolouration of the fly-leaves are in almost mint condition.

Burnard kept the text of his books to a minimum, using only sufficient words to amplify the information given by his photographs. Thus, Volume I consists of about 60 pages of text and 15 full page photographs, plus a number of sketches. Volumes II and III are similar in content, but Volume IV has rather more pages of text—84, and has 19 full page photographs as well as sketches and a number of helpful diagrams. The latter volume is largely devoted to a description of the prehistoric remains on Dartmoor and gives details of some of the archaeological investigations in which the author was involved from the 1890's onward.

But it is in the illustrations that these books excel. These are mostly reproductions of photographs taken by the author himself. They are all of Dartmoor subjects and range widely over and around the Moor—houses and farms, bridges, streams, tors, prehistoric and other archaeological remains, all are there. There is even a photograph of Jonas Coaker, the Dartmoor poet, who Burnard obviously knew well. Also, every now and again one comes across a tiny line drawing of some item that has attracted the author's notice, for examples, a sketch of the tinners' mould in the Higher Blowing House, on the Walkham (in Volume III) and a delightful vignette of the ancient gatehouse of Tavistock Abbey (in Volume I). The photographs are clearly the work of a master of his craft; in fact their texture and depth and clarity are almost incredible considering that it is now nearly a century since they were first published. The skill of this photographer certainly arouses my envy—no bald-headed skies for Robert Burnard.

Anyone into whose possession Burnard's masterpieces come must soon be aware that the author was a man of many talents and above all that he was a great lover of Dartmoor—this indeed he was, as his life's history shows. This is not the place for a complete review of Burnard's life and works, but just a few comments may not be out of place. One would wish to know, for example, how his association with Dartmoor came about. We are told that Robert Burnard was born in 1848, the son of a Plymouth businessman who specialised in the manufacture and sale of chemical and other fertilisers. Burnard entered his father's business and achieved considerable success. He is said to have taken a great interest in the water-borne deposits brought down by the river Plym and which settled in the vicinity of the family wharfs. These deposits contained material associated with the ancient tin mining industry on Dartmoor and his search for information about this, it is said, brought him to the Moor. He quickly became interested in the many other aspects of Dartmoor but particularly in its antiquities and their preservation. He was a founder member of the Dartmoor Preservation Association, which came into existence in 1883 and was particularly concerned about the preservation of the right of public access to the Moor. But it was in connection with his association with the Devonshire Association (the Devonshire

55

Association for the Advancement of Science, Literature and Art, to give it its full title) for which he is best remembered. Burnard was an early member of the Barrow Committee of the Association and later of the Dartmoor Exploration Committee. He is credited with having been one of the first persons to systematically excavate the Dartmoor hut circles. In these activities he was associated with such outstanding figures as Sabine Baring-Gould and Richard Hansford Worth. While it is true that these Dartmoor stalwarts did not always agree with the actions and theories of one another they were a formidable and far seeing trio. The work of their hands and the effects of their influence is still plainly visible on the Dartmoor scene. Some of the views they expressed may seem strange to us in 1986 and not all their methods of excavation would be acceptable today. But for all that it is clear that they, and Burnard in particular, were long-headed, deep thinking and sensitive men and Dartmoor lovers today have much to thank them for.

Robert Burnard was a pioneer in another way also. He is credited with having been one of the very first persons to have expressed the opinion that Dartmoor should become a public park. This was in 1894 and he advocated that it should come under the control of the County Council. The seed of this idea germinated and took root and in 1951 the Dartmoor National Park came into existence, largely under the aegis of the County Council. I doubt very much whether Burnard would be entirely pleased with the National Park as it is today, but I am sure he would acknowledge that what we have is much better that what we would have had if the National Parks Act had never been passed.

Burnard died in 1920, long before his great idea bore fruit. That he is so well remembered and so often spoken of by people who are concerned about Dartmoor is a great and lasting tribute to his genius and single-mindedness.

FURTHER READING:

Burnard's full obituary notice will be found in *Vol. 52 (1920) of the Transactions of the Devonshire Association*, page 37. In this notice details of his many contributions to the pages of the Transactions will also be found.

13

BRIDESTOWE

Of all the thirty-five or so villages whose parishes extend around the perimeter of Dartmoor, Bridestowe is, I suppose, one of the least visited and least appreciated. The reason is not far to seek, for the village itself is now about two miles distant from the edge of the Moor and is separated from it by the A.386 road. But this was not always so, as a glance at a large scale map will reveal. This seems to me to be one of those areas where the moorland has receded and the land been enclosed and put under the plough in the last few centuries. Indeed there are still large areas of land within the parish and in the neighbouring parish of Sourton which would be indistinguishable from moorland were it not for the fact that they are surrounded by enclosed land. For examples, Fernworthy Down in Bridestowe and Sourton Down in Sourton. The identity of this formerly moorland terrain has recently been more strongly emphasised by the discovery of previously unrecognised features which seem to be prehistoric remains similiar to those found in such large numbers on Dartmoor proper. Notice too that Bridestowe shares with its neighbour Sourton a huge area of common land to the east of the A.386 road. These commons, shown on the O.S. maps as "Lands Common to the Parishes of Bridestowe and Sourton (Bridestowe and Sourton Common)", are genuine Dartmoor moorland and indeed, on the eastern side have a common boundary with the Forest of Dartmoor.

As to the village of Bridestowe itself, this can be reached either by way of a lane, two miles long, which comes off the A.386 Tavistock to Okehampton road, opposite the Fox and Hounds, or by way of a side road which leaves the A.30 about $2\frac{1}{2}$ miles south-west of Sourton Cross. If the first mentioned route is chosen the visitor passes the site of the old Bridestowe railway station, now a private residence, where the passenger footbridge over the line forms an unusual feature in the

Bridestowe—the village centre.

garden. Near this point also is the spot where the long defunct Rattlebrook Peat Railway joined the main line.

Once the village is reached the reason for my interest in it becomes obvious. Bridestowe is not a large village, but it is clean and neat and has several attractive features. These include a number of beautiful old cottages, two pleasant pubs and an ancient bridge where the Crandford Brook passes under the road. As is usual with Dartmoor villages its principal feature is the church. This is quite large for the size of the community it serves; it is built of granite and has a typical Dartmoor tower with four crockets. The interior is somewhat plain, having been drastically restored in the 19th century. But it is nevertheless a cool and pleasant place and clearly lovingly tended. The church is dedicated to St. Brigid, an early Irish saint, and this indeed is the reason for the name of the village, i.e. Bridestowe, the stow or church of St. Brigid. There are three entrances to the churchyard, but one of them is of special note. Here the visitor enters under an ancient granite arch, adjacent to the old almshouses. It transpires that the arch was part of a former church and was pulled down and re-erected here when the building was restored. But what

Bridestowe Church.

Altar tombs, Bridestowe churchyard.

59

pleases me most about the churchyard is the collection of splendid old altar tombs which will be found quite near the south door of the church. There are six of these, all of 18th century date. They are built from a variety of clearly local materials, granite, slate and in one case red brick. All but one have inscriptions—the exception is a tomb with a huge granite slab which plainly once had an inscribed panel of slate, now missing. The tomb that fascinated me most is the grave of William and Martha Gubbins. Martha died 21st July, 1793, and William on 20th June the following year, aged 80. The slab bears the following inscription: *"Near 50 years of mortal life, we were a happy man and wife. The nights are past, the stars remain. So those who die shall live again."*

Apart from the beauty and dignity of their tomb the surname of this old couple aroused my interest. Dartmoor lovers will remember the old stories about the band of outlaws who lived in holes and caves in this part of the world; some accounts say that Lydford Gorge was their stronghold. We seem to know very little about these people, except that their surname was Gubbins. They are said to have lived around the 16th and 17th centuries and it will be remembered that in Charles Kingsley's famous novel *"Westward Ho!"* the author stages an encounter—and a fight—between his hero Salvation Yeo and the chief of the Gubbinses. I have been able to trace only two first-hand references to the Gubbins tribe, both by writers who were living in the early and mid-17th century. The first of these is our old friend William Browne of Tavistock, author of *"Brittania's Pastorals"*, which is a very long poem indeed, and of *"Lydford Journey"*, otherwise *"Lydford Law"*, for which he is very much better known (in Devon at least) today. In the latter work Browne devotes two verses to the Gubbinses, thus:

> "And near hereto's the Gubbins cave;
> A people that no knowledge have
> Of law, of God, or men:
> Whom Caesar never yet subdued;
> Who've lawless lived; of manners rude;
> All savage in their den."

> "By whom if any pass that way,
> He dares not the least time to stay,
> For presently they howl;

Upon which signal they do muster
Their naked forces in a cluster,
Led forth by Roger Rowle."

Rowle was apparently the leader of this lawless gang.

Browne apparently felt, being a local man, that the Gubbinses were well enough known for it to be unnecessary for him to dwell upon their misdeeds. But the other author referred to, Thomas Fuller by name, had rather more to say about them. Fuller was a clergyman who, it appears, got himself into trouble with the Parliamentarians and was in consequence deprived of his benefice. He was not a Devonian but spent two or three years in the county, at Exeter. Fuller was an inveterate writer and seems to have put down on paper everything that interested him. In a treatise which he called *"The Wonders of the County of Devon"*, Fuller described the Gubbinses and their mode of life at length. In brief, he says that they lived near Brentor, and that, among other things, they dwelt "in cotts (rather holes than houses) like swine, having everything in common", including their wives. Without marriage, says Fuller, they had multiplied into many hundreds. Their language was "the dregs of the dross of the vulgar Devonian", which it seems no-one but themselves could understand. They lived by stealing sheep off the Moor and it was beyond the power of authority to bring them to book. So you see, they were socialists, adulterers and sheep stealers too. No wonder they were outlaws.

It occurred to me that it might be interesting to try and find out whether any of the descendants of the original Gubbinses were still to be found in the vicinity. I confess that I did not carry this research to its ultimate end, but I did discover that there was at that time no resident of the name to be found on the Electoral Roll for the parish of Bridestowe. I also found out that the name Gubbins and its variant Gubbin are fairly common in Cornwall and that a few people with these names reside in Plymouth. Whether they are descended from our Gubbinses who can say? By the way, the authorities say that the name is derived from Gilbert and its variant Gibb. Gilbert means a person who gives gifts to his friends and Gibb is also a nickname for a cat— take your choice!

Some of us too remember that Nathaniel Gubbins was the pen-name of a popular and amusing columnist in the old days of the *Sunday Express*.

14

WHAT DO YOU THINK THIS IS?

Once he has developed what I call the "seeing eye", the Dartmoor explorer will find that he often comes across some artefact, or building or other feature which is puzzling because of its shape or size or apparent irrelevance to its immediate surroundings. As the years go by and his knowledge of the Moor and its history increases many of these features will be explained, either by reading or talking to knowledgeable people. Sometimes sheer cerebral activity will produce an acceptable theory which in the absence of pure fact suffices as a working hypothesis. But at the end of the day, perhaps after many years, a few of these moorland puzzles remain just that. I can think of two which fall into this category; one remains just as mysterious today as it was when it first came to my notice. The other has now been explained—to my satisfaction at least—but only very recently, whilst I have been writing this book. Before describing these however I will deal with a number of others for which satisfactory explanations have been forthcoming.

Many years ago I saw in the farmyard of a farm at Ilsington, a flat square slab of granite. It was about 15 inches square and about 5 inches thick. It had been carefully worked, the upper surface was slightly dished in the centre and the slab was perforated by five round holes each about an inch in diameter. What was it? The farmer provided the answer—he was in a favourable position, for his family has farmed this same farm for over 300 years. "Oh", he said, "that is a drainhole cover. It is probably 150 years old, or more." And he went on to say that in view of the skilled workmanship the cover had probably been made by a master stone-mason working in or near the Haytor Quarries. Quite soon after this incident I came across another very

62

Granite drainhole cover, Ilsington.

Section of an apple mill, Belstone Common.

similar but larger cover, in the grounds of an hotel at Bovey Tracey. The proprietor had no idea what the object might be, but I was pleased to be able to enlighten him.

On the forecourt of the post office in the moorland hamlet where I live will be seen a block of granite about 18 inches tall and perhaps 15 inches in diameter. It has been worked into a roughly cylindrical shape and a slot, about 5 inches wide and 4 inches deep has been cut across the top from side to side. This slot is deeper in the centre than at the sides, with the result that water stands in it. Round holes have been bored in the top of the block, one on either side of the slot, and in one of them an iron lug with a loop has been leaded into the granite. This was obviously matched by a similar one on the other side, but unfortunately the granite around the hole has broken away and this lug is missing. The whole thing probably weighs about 200 lbs. Clearly this carefully worked piece of rock had some special purpose, but what was it? I recognised it at once when I first saw it, but then, I was at an advantage because I had seen something similar, but fixed, not portable as this is, on a Dartmoor farm in the Plym valley. It is in fact the base of a grindstone. The lugs with loops were the bearings which took the axle of the grindstone; one side of the axle would be fitted

Granite base of a grindstone—Haytor Vale.

with a crank handle, like the starting handle of a motor car. The grindstone itself (it is missing of course) would have been of fine sandstone, probably about 7 in. in diameter, and it would have revolved in water placed in the cavity at the base of the slot, to prevent the stone from overheating and spoiling the tool being sharpened. The whole thing would probably have stood upon a block of wood or something similar and would have been used to sharpen small tools—billhooks, slashers and the like. How old? almost any age I suppose, but probably of 19th century vintage. Such grindstones are seldom used today.

When one remembers that with gaps because of changes in climate, Dartmoor has been home for farmers for at least four thousand years, it is not surprising that many remains of farming activities are still to be found upon the Moor. Farmers are severely practical people and generally speaking hate spending money on items of equipment that can be made or adapted from natural resources. This was particularly true in former days when money was scarce and needs simple. Because many of the items used in husbandry could be made from the native rock and because granite is a somewhat intractable rock and liable to "go wrong" when being worked there are many partly worked and abandoned examples to be found lying about. Add to these the items that were satisfactorily completed and which have survived and their tally is indeed tremendous. Many of the latter are still in daily use; for example slotted gateposts, now fitted with iron hinges and catches, which formerly carried the five separate bars of the original five-barred gate. How many great and small granite troughs can you find around almost any moorland farm? Some of these must be centuries old and some of them, the larger ones, were almost certainly vats which held cider in the days when every farm had its cider press. Some farm troughs started off in life as tinners' moulds, but that is another story. Circular troughs of various sizes but each with a raised boss in the centre, formerly in use as the poundstones of an apple mill, but now doing humble service as pig troughs, are often found—and they make splendid bird-baths and flower beds of course. But here and there something even more interesting comes to notice. Standing on a wall near the ancient longhouse at Sanders, Lettaford (near North Bovey), is a small carefully worked circular granite trough. It is about ten inches in diameter and the cut out trough section is perhaps three or four inches deep. A section of the side wall has been cut out so as to form a spout or lip. This object is the bottom part of a hand-mill or

Granite quern or hand mill—Bagtor, Ilsington.

quern, used in the days when small quantities of grain, wheat perhaps, or more likely barley, were ground at home to make bread. It must be remembered that farmers and their families occupying Dartmoor farms led very isolated lives and had to be very largely self sufficient. A visit to a distant mill would probably occupy the best part of a day, whereas the use of a hand-mill at home would involve only one female member of the family for a short time. A quern consisted of two parts; one, the base or pound-stone, as in the specimen described at Lettaford, and the other, the upper-stone, which was in fact the grinding medium. The upper-stone is a disc of stone shaped to fit inside the pound-stone; known specimens are usually between two and four inches thick and have two or more holes in the upper surface to enable a handle or stick to be used to impart a circular motion to the stone. A metal distance piece is fitted inside the pound-stone and upon this the upper-stone revolves. The corn to be ground was placed in the pound-stone, the upper was then put in place and rotated, thus grinding the grain to flour. The flour emerged from the spout or lip and was caught in a receptacle placed for the purpose. Many examples of querns can be seen around the Moor, usually in old farmyards or in use as garden ornaments, but usually only the pound-stone is present. Upper stones are rare; they are comparatively fragile and liable to accidental breakage and few seem to have survived. If you should come across one, even a broken or damaged specimen, please do all you can to ensure its safe keeping and report its existence to the National Park Archaeologist.

Another kind of artefact of which many specimens exist is a cylinder of granite, ten or twelve inches in diameter and varying in length from roughly five feet to about 12 inches. If the specimen is complete it will probably be fitted with iron stub-axles a few inches in length at either end. Broken examples are often found. If the roller—for that is what it is—is more than about 18 inches long it was almost certainly an agricultural implement known as a flat-roll. These were used in connection with the growing of grain crops. After the seed grain had germinated, the roll, drawn by a horse (or oxen perhaps) was passed over the crop so as to firm the ground and at the same time press the infant plant into the soil. This induced the sideways growth known as "tillering" and ensured a better crop. The same technique is still used on farms today of course, but rollers these days are made of iron and pulled by tractors. But there are many granite rollers still to be found around Dartmoor farms, sometimes just abandoned and sometimes in use as gateposts or performing other useful functions.

Shorter granite rollers are often found, say 15 to 18 inches long. These, if complete and not broken sections of an agricultural implement were probably once part of an apple mill. Before apples can be made into cider they must first be pulped. This used to be achieved by putting the apples into the kind of circular trough with a raised boss in the centre, as described earlier. The pulping was done by trundling a stone wheel, called the edge-runner, around the inside of the trough until the apples were sufficiently crushed. Later a more sophisticated type of mill was introduced. This was usually installed on the ground floor of a building known as the pound-house. The apples were poured down a chute into the mill, which consisted of two or more revolving stone rollers. When the rollers had reduced the apples to a pulp it was pressed between layers of straw to express the juice which ran into a great stone vat for fermentation. The power for these apple mills was usually a horse or pony walking in a perpetual circle. Thus the pound-house was also often a round house and many of these can be seen among the buildings of Dartmoor border farms. The cog wheels and gearing connected with these mills were often made of wood and so have not survived. But the stone components, i.e. the pound-stones, edge-runners, rollers (sometimes with lengthwise grooves cut in them), troughs and vats are often found, still serving in other ways. So too are the flat, more or less circular slabs of granite, with runnels cut in the upper surface and connected with a lip at one side, which formed the base of the actual press. There is a particularly fine specimen of the latter kind at Longstone Island, Burrator.

Many of the short granite rollers described above were later furnished with iron frames and handles and became garden rollers, and these are quite common even today.

It should be noted too that stone artefacts, mainly of granite, were more often than not made in situ on the Moor, from moorstone, as the unquarried granite is called. The unreliable nature of granite for making artefacts has already been mentioned. Because of this idiosyncrasy many items were spoiled in the making and hundreds of abandoned specimens of many different kinds can be found scattered over the length and breadth of Dartmoor. But in some areas so many partly made objects with no visible fault can be found that it seems likely that someone was engaged in making them hoping for orders for the finished product which never materialised. On the slopes below Haytor Rocks, for instance, may be found several partly worked millstones or edge-runners, one almost finished. And the valley of the Steeperton Brook is another place where a similar profusion exists.

For hundreds of years and up until the beginning of the present century, Dartmoor farmers not only had the right to take surface stone from the Moor for their own purposes, but actually made from moorstone many objects which could more conveniently have been made from wood or iron. But the stone was free, the farmer had the skill to work it, labour was cheap and cost was a very important factor. Hence the great profusion of stone artefacts to be found around the Moor today.

It is not possible, within the scope of a chapter in a book like this to deal with every different kind of item that the observant explorer may find. I hope that enough has been said to explain the purpose of just a few of these objects and perhaps to stimulate the curiosity of people who have not so far taken an interest in such matters. But now, back to the two mysterious items that I mentioned earlier.

The first of these will be found partly built into the bank of a disused leat on Buckfastleigh Moor, a hundred yards or so from and to the west of the moor gate at Lyd Gate. (Approx. at G.R. 682673.) The object

Dartmoor mystery? This stone is built into the bank of a dry leat near Lud Gate, Buckfastleigh Moor.

in question consists of a slab of granite, about 44 inches square and $9\frac{1}{2}$ inches thick. This massive slab—it must weigh well over a quarter of a ton—is perforated through the centre by a rectangular hole 15 inches by 13. It has been carefully worked by someone who was clearly a skilled stone mason. It was brought to my notice by a friend who thought it might possibly be the base of a cross. On seeing it I thought so too, but close examination showed that the inner side of the socket bears the marks of the drill. This enables us to say that it is unlikely to have been made earlier than the beginning of the 19th century. By this time wayside crosses were no longer being erected on Dartmoor. It seemed unlikely that a cross intended for erection elsewhere would have been made actually on the Moor at so late a date, though this is not of course impossible. Another similar slab, but not so finely worked and without the perforation, lies a few yards away.

Now began an elaborate game of conjecture; we discussed this matter with many people and various suggestions were made as to its purpose. One friend suggested that it might have been intended for use in the rebuilding of Buckfast Abbey and another that it might have something to do with the disused Huntingdon tin mine, which is only

69

about a mile away to the west. But nothing positive. Eventually I mentioned the matter to my friend Edward Masson Phillips and from him came the first real information. It seems that in the early 1930's Mr Masson Phillips was engaged in the researching and writing of his masterly work on the Ancient Stone Crosses of Devon. The late Richard Hansford Worth reported to him that he had found the perforated slab described above and another that we have so far been unable to find. Both slabs were built into the banks of leats when Worth found them and in his notes he described them as "water regulating stones for leat". Worth's notes are accompanied by sketches of the two stones he found and in each case the sketches show two small round holes bored in the granite, side by side below the central rectangular hole. These could very well have been intended to accept iron bolts. We cannot confirm the existence of these holes, excavation would be needed.

I have the geatest respect for any opinion advanced by R. H. Worth. Not only was he the foremost authority upon Dartmoor of his day, but he was a civil engineer by profession and skilled in water engineering. On the other hand I was reluctant to accept his identification of these stones as water regulators because of their size and shape. There are scores of leats on Dartmoor, active and disused, and many of these have regulating stones—known as bullseyes—at points where side channels go off to provide water for some subsidiary purpose. But the holes in the bullseyes that I know are all circular in shape and no more than two or three inches in diameter. The square hole in our stone is very large in comparison, and the trouble involved in cutting a large square hole like this instead of one or more smaller round ones must have been tremendous. So further investigation was called for. We started by following the dry leat, into the bank of which our stone has been built, and soon found that it is part of a network of dry channels each of which clearly served some individual purpose in former times. Our dry channel eventually led us to a point at which it had been taken off the Hayford Leat, still in use, which comes off the Western Wella Brook near Huntingdon Warren and supplies water to the farm at Hayford. We noted at least two other dry side channels en route.

Shortly after the expedition described in the last paragraph we learned that another stone similar to the one we already knew about had been found, on private land this time, but again built into the bank of a dry leat associated with the Hayford Leat. Furthermore we learned that our friend who started this particular hare running had found someone who remembered the Hayford Leat in the days when its various branches were operative and who knew that the stones described by Worth were indeed "water regulating stones for the leat". It seems that in those days the leat served not only Hayford itself, but two other residences, plus a sawmill and a tin mine, the latter on Wallaford Down. The stone near Lyd Gate controlled the water supply for Furze Acres, a house only a couple of hundred yards away. There seems to be no doubt that Worth was right.

Readers fortunate enough to possess a copy of the Rev. Hugh Breton's little book *The Forest of Dartmoor. Pt. 1,* published in 1931 will find that on page 17 he refers to a similar stone that he found and identified as the base of a cross, at the corner of Hayford Plantation, about half a mile from Lyd Gate. We have searched for this and for Worth's second stone which he described as being on Lydgate Plains, i.e., the more or less level area of moorland to the north and north-west of the moor gate, but so far have not found them. You may be more fortunate.

Another Dartmoor mystery.

My second, and so far unsolved mystery, concerns two blocks of granite, rather like short gateposts, each about five feet long, lying alongside one another but inclined at an angle from each other. At one end of the upper surface of each of these blocks are three round holes, each about an inch in diameter. The holes are connected by deep V shaped grooves or slots cut in the granite. The blocks lie in the bottom of a shallow tinners' gully on Bush Down, a couple of hundred yards or so NE of Warren House Inn, north of the road. The gully could have been the course of a light tramway connected with the old Bush Down Mine, and the blocks could have been part of the points system of the possible tramway. But someone else has conjectured that they might have been part of some kind of a vermin trap—so what were they?

NOTES.

If this aspect of Dartmoor lore interests you you should read the chapter entitled *"The Moorstone Age"* in R. H. Worth's *"Dartmoor"* (page 355), published by David & Charles.

E. N. Masson Phillips' work on *"The Ancient Stone Crosses of Devon"* is to be found in the *Transactions of the Devonshire Association, Vols. LXIX(1937) and LXX(1938)*. There are supplementary reports on the same subject in the volumes for 1939, 1940, 1943, 1954, 1959, 1979 and 1984. These volumes can be found in the larger reference libraries in the County.

The upper stone of a quern, albeit broken, can be seen in the museum at Totnes.

15

HAYTOR VALE

Haytor Vale is of course, the valley which lies at the southern foot of Haytor Down, about a mile to the east of the famous Haytor Rocks from which the Vale takes its name. The valley gives rise to the Liverton Brook which flows through the Vale, past Smallacombe Farm and on to join the River Teign not far from Teigngrace. Today Haytor Vale could best be described as a nuclear hamlet. It is home for a population of a hundred or so people who live in the forty or fifty houses which cluster around the Rock Inn, which in the absence of a church does duty as the focal centre of the community. The parish Church, St. Michael's, is about a mile and a half away in the parent village of Ilsington. The parish of Ilsington is very extensive, extending as it does from the top of Widecombe Hill to the outskirts of Highweek, next door to Newton Abbot, a distance of something like seven miles, as the crow flies.

Around the perimeter of the Vale lies the district known simply as Haytor, which itself houses a sizeable community, also part of Ilsington parish. This area has no nuclear centre and so its inhabitants tend to gravitate towards Ilsington village or Haytor Vale according to distance and personal preference.

The visitor wandering around the Vale and looking for local colour will quickly discover that there are very few ancient or even old buildings to be found, most of the dwellings are comparatively modern; a few date from the turn of the century but many are of quite recent date. The fact is that Haytor Vale's very existence was originally based upon the Haytor granite quarries, which were opened in the late 18th or early 19th century. The oldest buildings are the Rock Inn and the dozen cottages in the midst of which it stands. The inn and the cottages were built by the proprietor of the quarries, George Templer, to house his labour force about 1826 and to provide them with relaxation. There were originally 24 cottages, back to back, and it is on record that the rent for these was 1s 6d a week for a front cottage and 1s 3d for one at the back. The cottages were known as "The Buildings" and the inn as "The Rock Hotel". The name "Haytor Vale" is itself of quite modern vintage; in a reference in *Murray's* *"Guide to Devon and Cornwall"* dated 1859 the place is called "the hamlet of Heytor Town". "Town" of course being the modern equivalent of the Saxon "tun"—a settlement.

Despite what has been said about the lack of ancient buildings there are, nevertheless, indications of earlier occupation in the Vale. On the hillside which slopes down to the Vale from the north there are a number of little fields known to this day and named on the map as "the Shotts". It is thought by competent historians that these little fields were taken in from the common perhaps three or more centuries ago and that they were perhaps part of a small-holding whose farmhouse stood nearby. No trace of this exists today but the theory seems reasonable and probable. It is known that the land in the Vale was formerly part of the Smallacombe estate, the ancient farmstead of which lies half a mile or so to the south-east.

Haytor Vale has another claim to fame besides its association with the Haytor granite quarries. This lies in the fact that at the south-eastern end of the vale lies the site of the Haytor Iron Mine. Signs of this exist in the shape of an immense pit, now rapidly being filled in, on the right of the road going south and a very large and high spoil heap, between the pit just mentioned and the Women's Institute Hut. Formerly there were two other great pits, now both filled in. These pits and the spoil heap were the site of the open-cast workings of the iron mine. A walk of two or three hundred yards along the public footpath which runs behind the Rock Inn will bring the visitor to a point where the path branches. At this spot, on the right, will be seen a padlocked door at the foot of the cliff. This door gives access to the underground workings of the same mine. These workings are now largely flooded and no access for the public is possible.

It seems that magnetic iron ore and brown haematite were mined at Haytor from an early date, perhaps as early as the 16th century, but of this no record has yet been found. It is known however that when the mining of iron ore began, probably in the 1820's, signs of ancient workings were found which indicated that this was not the first time that the ore had been worked. In passing it may be noted that the earliest type of navigational compass, in use from the 13th century, consisted of a splinter of magnetite (magnetic iron ore or lodestone) floating on a bowl of water. Many of the old topographers refer to lodestones being found in Devon, but none mentions Haytor. The Haytor Iron Mine worked intermittently from the early 19th century with long gaps between periods of activity until it finally closed down in 1921. One drawback to the industry was the fact that the ore had to be sent to Wales or elsewhere to be smelted, because of lack of suitable fuel locally. At one period attempts were made to smelt the fuel "on site" using lignite (brown coal) from Bovey Tracey as fuel. This attempt failed because the lignite would not produce sufficient heat unless it had first been turned into charcoal and this proved unsatisfactory. Transport too was difficult despite the use of a traction engine to convey the ore to the railhead by road. At one time the mine owners entered into an arrangement which permitted them to have their ore conveyed on the Haytor granite tramway which ran within a quarter of a mile of the mine. How much use was made of this facility is not known, but in any case the tramway itself ceased to operate by 1858 and the granite quarries closed down in the 1880's.

Until just a few years ago the name of the famous rock, and the district around it, was spelled "Heytor" by most people. Today that form has almost entirely disappeared, probably because local people no longer speak with the local intonation nearly as much as formerly. Also of course many more people use maps and the Ordnance Survey have favoured the present form of the name during pretty well the whole of the present century. But what does the name mean? The earliest reference that I can find which undoubtedly relates to the place in question is dated 1566. This referred not to the famous rocks, or to the Vale, but to the down or common, which at that time was Idetordoune. Later spellings were Ittor Doune (1687), Idetor (1737), Eator Down (1762) and Itterdown (1789). By the end of the 18th century it was being called High Torr down, and there are a number of other and some later variations. But there seems to be no doubt that the Haytor of today is the high tor of yesterday, the lofty rock pile that could be seen for many miles from the north and east and south. As indeed it still can today.

16

"THAT WHICH WAS LOST IS FOUND AGAIN"

In my *"Dartmoor Crosses and Some Ancient Tracks"*, which came out in 1983, I commented that a cross described by both William Crossing and E. N. Masson Phillips as standing at the roadside near Elsford Farm, between Hennock and Moretonhampstead, could not now be found. This statement intrigued a friend of mine, Ernest Ilieve, (now unhappily deceased) who lived not far away, and he decided to look for himself. His efforts were rewarded, as mine had not been, and he eventually discovered the cross which over the years had been covered over with roadside debris and was completely hidden from view. Ernest removed the covering and the cross, a mere remnant of what was once a massive granite monument, is now plain for all to see. The remnant consists of the head and arms (one arm is badly broken) and a short piece of the shaft. The whole thing stands about 23 inches high and is 31 inches across the arms. It is of somewhat rude construction and is typical of the kind of wayside cross we find around the Dartmoor borders. We know nothing of the age or history of this cross but it seems pretty certain that its original position was at or near where it now stands and that it marked the track to the churchtown— Moreton or Hennock—long before the track became a road; perhaps as early as the 13th century. The cross stands at GR 792829, on the north side of the road right opposite the entrance to Lower Elsford Farm.

Also in *"Dartmoor Crosses"* I referred to a cross shaft and socket stone then lying by the roadside in the lane leading to Walkhampton Church. Since I wrote, in 1984 in fact, the shaft and socket have been brought together and erected opposite the ancient Church House,

Elford Cross, Hennock.

near which they were found. This restoration was financed by the generosity of Mrs Helen Andrew, who formerly lived at Ward House, nearby. It will be noticed that the socket stone of this cross is triangular in shape and very rough of construction. I am quite sure in my own mind that in its original condition the socket stone would have been below ground level and not on view as it is in its restored form. Sockets of this kind, where the shaft actually penetrates the socket, are fairly common in the Dartmoor district. The shaft in question is of granite. It is of octagonal section and something over five feet tall and it has the remains of an iron gate or door catch embedded in it. Nothing is known of the whereabouts of the head of this cross and nothing of its original site or purpose; it may have been the churchyard cross from the nearby church or a wayside cross marking the route to the church or the monks' path to Buckland Abbey, not far away. The shaft and socket are so different in type and construction that I think it unlikely that they originally formed part of the same cross. One final point on this subject. I have seen a

The Church House, Walkhampton.
(restored cross shaft and base far right).

Restored cross shaft and base, Walkhampton Church.

drawing by Samuel Prout of early 19th century date which shows quite clearly the shaft referred to above forming part of a lean-to building at the eastern end of the Walkhampton Church House. This building has now disappeared.

The Church House at Walkhampton is a truly beautiful old building, probably of 16th century origin. When it ceased to be used for its original purposes it served a number of other uses; it was a public house for some time and ceased to be so used in 1855. The building has now been beautifully restored and is a delightful and picturesque dwelling. Walkhampton Church and Church House are both about half a mile from the village of the same name and stand close together. It is possible to visit them by car but the best way to get at them is to park somewhere convenient and approach on foot through the lanes. Explorers who do this may reap the additional reward of discovering Well Town, where there is a small colony of splendid ancient buildings with the public road running through what used to be the farm yard. Well Town lies about a quarter of a mile to the east of the church.

Also in "*Crosses*" I devoted some space to speculating about what might have happened to the original Hobajon's Cross, today represented by a stone post inscribed with a cross and standing in a row of boundary stones marking the Harford/Ugborough parish boundary. I would dearly love to be able to claim that Hobajon's Cross had been found again, but this I cannot do. Something has come up however and it ought to be mentioned because of the confusion that could otherwise arise. Some considerable time ago my friend Harry Davies of North Tawton told me that he had found a stone, which he thought might be a cross, standing in the line of boundary stones that extends northward from Three Barrows. He produced a photograph of what certainly resembled a cross, and a map. The map was an early printing of the Ordnance Survey's First Series 1:25000 ($2\frac{1}{2}$ inches to the mile) map of Brent Moor and vicinity (Sheet No. SX 66). This map showed Hobajon's Cross standing, not in its present place, more than a mile to the south of Three Barrows, but in the line of boundary stones about a quarter of a mile north of Three Barrows. It was here that the supposed cross had been found by Harry. Not unnaturally this intrigued me very much and I made an early opportunity to visit the spot. Yes, there stood a stone which viewed from some angles certainly had something of the appearance of a cross, albeit a very crude cross and unfinished at that, one arm being completely

79

Boundary stone or cross?   **Photograph by A. H. D. Davies.**
North of Three Barrows, S. Dartmoor.

unformed. But close examination proved, to my satisfaction at least, that this piece of rock had never received the attentions of a serious worker in stone. To me it appeared as though someone, perhaps the workmen who erected the boundary stone, saw some resemblance to a cross in the stone they were about to erect and improved the shining hour by knocking a few additional pieces off with a hammer. The broken edges of the stone were quite clean and sharp and showed no sign of the weathering which is always present on ancient stone artefacts found on Dartmoor. So no, it isn't Hobajon's Cross but just a boundary stone. The Ordnance Survey have obviously recognised their mistake and on later maps Hobajon's Cross is back again where it has been shown for many years. But it was a good try and we all got something out of it, if only a good walk and food for more speculation.

In *"Odds & Ends from Dartmoor"*, published in 1984, I devoted a chapter to Rock Basins, Tolmens and Logan Stones and commented that several of these natural objects had been damaged or had disappeared altogether in recent years. In the latter category I put the great Drewsteignton Logan in the bed of the Teign between Fingle Bridge and Dogamarsh Bridge, which I had never been able to find. No

The Drewsteignton Logan Stone, from a sketch by Samuel Prout dated 1806.

sooner was the book in print than my friend and fellow author Brian Le Messurier got in touch to say that the Drewsteignton Logan was still where it ought to be and that he had seen it only a few days before writing. Brian gave me such explicit directions that I was able to find the stone without further difficulty. It lies close to the left bank of the river on a bed of rock but not on an island as depicted in Prout's print of 1806. It is a block of rock about 7 feet tall and varying in thickness from about 5 feet to about 10 feet. I could not make it log at all. My difficulty in finding it was caused by its being obscured by the dense foliage of trees and shrubs nearby and the fact that the riverside path by which it could formerly be approached has almost entirely disappeared and has been replaced by another path higher up the bank. The rock can only be approached by a somewhat hazardous route down the steep bank below Hunts Tor (Hunter's Tor on the map) or an even more perilous scramble over the rocks on the edge of the river—not recommended unless the river is very low. But the logan can be seen quite clearly from the opposite bank, especially when the leaves on the trees have fallen.

INDEX